RANDOM HOUSE

SPOTLIGHT

ON

COMPUTER LITERACY

ELLEN RICHMAN

 RANDOM HOUSE SCHOOL DIVISION

Author: **Ellen Richman**

Project Editor: Lynne Lewin
Art Director: Walter Norfleet
Production Supervisor: Lenore Zani

Design Studio: Sulpizio Associates
Illustrations: Phil Landry, Jack Weaver

34567CI 54

SPOTLIGHT ON COMPUTER LITERACY

TABLE OF CONTENTS

Welcome to the World of Computers iv

UNIT 1

How Computers Work

Chapter 1   Computer Systems 1
Chapter 2   How a Computer Works 5
Chapter 3   Communicating with a Computer 8
Chapter 4   Input and Output 12
Chapter 5   Memory 20
Chapter 6   Central Processing Unit 24
Chapter 7   Chips and Bits and Bytes 29

UNIT 2

Computers in Our Lives

Chapter 8   From Abacus to IBM 37
Chapter 9   Four Generations of Modern Computers 44
Chapter 10 Computers Are Everywhere 51
Chapter 11 Other Computer Uses—and Misuses 64
Chapter 12 Computer Careers 69

UNIT 3

BASIC Programming

Chapter 13 Meet Your Computer Keyboard 75
Chapter 14 Say Hello to Your Computer 80
Chapter 15 Jumping Around 91
Chapter 16 Addresses 97
Chapter 17 Stringing Along 105
Chapter 18 Talking Back 111
Chapter 19 Computer Decisions 118
Chapter 20 Rolling the Dice 127
Chapter 21 Looping Around 135
Chapter 22 Finding the Facts 142
Chapter 23 Computer Art 148
Chapter 24 On Your Own 171

Glossary 175
Index 184

Welcome to the World of Computers

Have you met a computer recently? Chances are you have. If you have made a phone call, a computer helped to place the call. If you have played an electronic game, a computer kept score and helped control the action. If you have flown in an airplane, a computer helped the pilot fly the plane. Even as you read this book, keep in mind that the words you are reading were put into type by a computer.

Here is a list of statements about computers. Decide whether each statement is true or false.

What do you know about computers?

1. Computers are smarter than humans.
2. Computers have brains.
3. Some computers have feelings.
4. Computers can solve any problem.
5. You need to know a lot of science and math to use a computer.

If you decided that each statement is false, you are correct. Computers are *not* smarter than humans. Computers do *not* have brains or feelings. They *cannot* solve every problem. And you do *not* have to know a lot of science or math to use a computer.

Then what is a computer? What can it do? It is a machine that can handle large amounts of information and work with amazing speed. A computer is built to do these four jobs:

1. **Accept information.** You can put information into it. The information might be a collection of facts and figures and a set of instructions to the computer telling it what to do.
2. **Store the information.** It has a device called a memory that holds the information as long as you want it to.
3. **Process the information.** This means it does something with the information. It might do an addition problem or compare and sort the information.
4. **Give out the processed information.** It gives you the results of the processing, which are the results of the instructions to the computer.

Computers are designed to follow instructions from a human being. They can solve only the problems that people tell them to solve. Since people cannot solve *every* problem, neither can computers. To tell a computer what to do, you have to know what problem you want to solve and have a plan for solving it.

Since computers can't do anything without instructions from a human, what makes them so special? They can do some things better than humans. Computers calculate faster than humans. They are more accurate than humans. Computers can also store vast amounts of information, and they do not "forget" what they store. These kinds of qualities make computers wonderful tools to help people solve problems.

Computers have become important and valuable tools in today's world. Since they affect so many parts of our lives, it is important to be aware of how they are used and how they work.

The purpose of *Spotlight on Computer Literacy* is to start you on your way toward becoming computer literate. What is the meaning of "computer literacy?" A person is considered "literate" if he or she is educated or has knowledge or experience in certain areas. To be *computer* literate, you need to know about computers and have some experience in using them.

In this book you will be learning about computers. In the first unit you will learn about different types of computers. You will also learn about the parts of a computer and what makes computers work. In the second unit you will be looking at some historical inventions that led to the development of modern computers. You will be learning how computers are used in business and industry, in government, and in schools and homes. You will also be looking at what kinds of career opportunities computers have created. In the third unit you will learn how to write programs for a computer.

When you have covered these three main areas—how computers work, how computers affect your life, and programming a computer—you will have taken a big step toward becoming computer literate. Welcome to the world of computers!

UNIT 1
HOW COMPUTERS WORK

Chapter 1 | COMPUTER SYSTEMS

Computers come in many sizes and shapes. They range from very large computer systems called mainframe computers to small minicomputers to even smaller microcomputers.

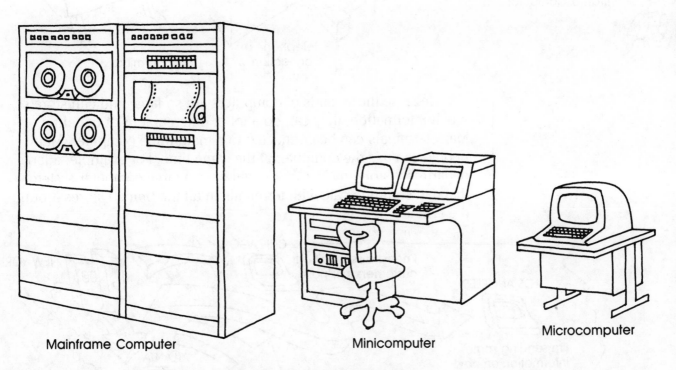

Mainframe Computer

Minicomputer

Microcomputer

Sometimes the ⇨ equipment fills several rooms.

Terminal means ⇨ "endpoint." A terminal is the "endpoint" of a computer system.

Mainframe computers are very large, often taking up as much space as a classroom. They can store enormous amounts of information. They cost hundreds of thousands of dollars. Some even cost more than a million dollars. Many large businesses, government agencies, and universities use mainframe computers to help them operate smoothly and efficiently. For example, a telephone company might use mainframe computers to keep track of all the long-distance calls its customers make. The U.S. Navy might use mainframes to help keep track of the movement and location of its ships and submarines. Universities use mainframes to schedule their students and record grades.

Mainframe computers often have many stations or **terminals** connected to them. These terminals look like small computers, but actually they are not. They are devices that send information to, and receive information from, the computer. Some terminals might be in the same room or building as the computer, and be connected to it with cables. Other terminals might be in another building or even in another city! These terminals "communicate" with the mainframe computer through telephone wires.

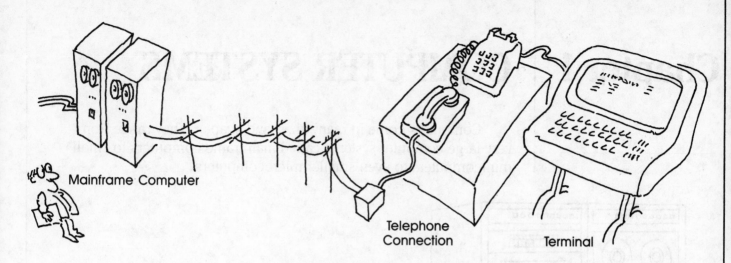

Mainframe Computer

Telephone Connection

Terminal

Because these kinds of computers are so large and can store so much information, they can do a lot of different jobs at one time. Many terminals can be connected to a mainframe computer. Many people can use the computer at the same time. For example, a large department store in New York might have a large computer system that can communicate with terminals in all the branch stores around the country.

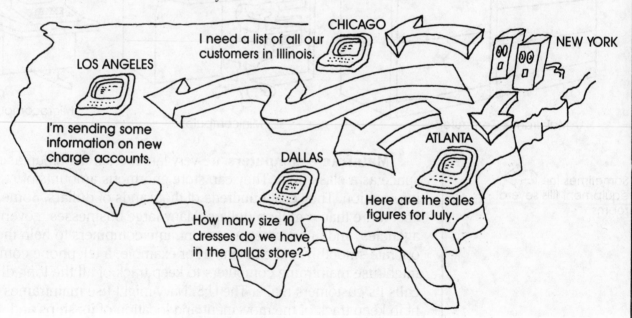

CHICAGO

I need a list of all our customers in Illinois.

NEW YORK

LOS ANGELES

I'm sending some information on new charge accounts.

ATLANTA

DALLAS

Here are the sales figures for July.

How many size 10 dresses do we have in the Dallas store?

Minicomputers are much smaller than mainframes. They take up only a small space on the floor. Some can even fit on a table. They range in cost from about 10 to 100 thousand dollars. They, too, can store large amounts of information, though not as much as mainframe computers. Like mainframes, minicomputers can handle more than one job at a time. They have terminals connected to them. Since they do not store as much information as mainframes, they have fewer terminals. They are used by medium and small companies as well as large companies. They are also used by some school systems.

In addition to using mainframe computers to handle information affecting the whole company, some large companies also use minicomputers in different departments. For example, most large banks have several departments—checking accounts, savings accounts, loans, international banking, and others. Each of these departments handles a lot of special information that does not concern other departments in the bank. So, rather than use the bank's mainframe system to handle this work, each department has its own minicomputer.

Checking Accounts

I need a bank statement for account number 478-37929.

Savings Accounts

How much interest on savings accounts did we pay out last year?

Loans

How much money did we loan for new cars this month?

International

I need to change the dollar amounts in this report to French Francs.

Some micros can be connected to mainframes through telephone hook-ups. Then the micro can be used as a terminal.

Remember, larger systems can do many jobs at one time.

Microcomputers are even smaller than minicomputers. They are often called "personal" or "home" computers because many people buy them for personal or home use. They are small and light enough to move around. They fit on a small table or desk. They usually cost less than $6000. In fact, many cost only a few hundred dollars. Microcomputers cannot store as much information as mainframes or minicomputers. Terminals cannot usually be connected to them.

Microcomputers are designed to do only one job at a time. Yet, they are used by large businesses as well as small businesses and offices. Although large businesses use mainframes and minicomputers to handle major computing chores, they often use microcomputers to help solve smaller, more individual problems. Many small businesses that cannot afford a large computer system find that a microcomputer fits their needs. It can be used for different kinds of jobs—though not at the same time. For example, a doctor's office may have a microcomputer that keeps track of the patients' accounts, prints bills, and schedules appointments.

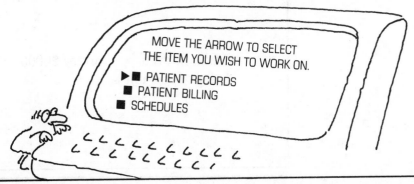

MOVE THE ARROW TO SELECT THE ITEM YOU WISH TO WORK ON.
► ■ PATIENT RECORDS
■ PATIENT BILLING
■ SCHEDULES

Many schools have microcomputers in their classrooms. Students can use computers to help them learn social studies, English, science, math, and other subjects. Teachers can use the computers to keep track of their students' progress or to do other kinds of record keeping. Some people have microcomputers in their homes to help them handle home finances, play computer games, or because they like to write programs as a hobby.

1. What kind of computer would you use for these jobs—mainframe computer, minicomputer, or microcomputer?

   a. A large city's electric company uses its computer to keep track of the amount of electricity used by thousands of customers each month.

   b. A person keeps recipes, important dates, and checking account records at home.

   c. A stockbroker uses a terminal to buy and sell stocks and bonds through a computer in the New York Stock Exchange.

   d. A computer at NASA headquarters is used for launching and tracking hundreds of satellites circling the earth.

   e. A bookkeeper in a large medical clinic uses a terminal to enter patients' bills into the clinic's computer.

2. Below is a summary of the three main kinds of computer systems. Tell the name of each system.

Size	Approximate Cost	Features
a. Can fill a room.	Hundreds of thousands to over a million dollars	Can do many jobs at once; can have many terminals; used by large businesses, government agencies, and universities.
b. Stands on floor or on a large table.	$10,000–$100,000	Can do several jobs at once; may have several terminals; used by medium and small businesses and individual departments in large companies.
c. Can fit on a desk (portable).	under $6000	Can do one job at a time; used by small businesses, for single jobs in larger companies, in homes, and in school classrooms.

Chapter 2

HOW A COMPUTER WORKS

Do you remember the ⇨
four jobs a computer
does?
Look at page iv.

When a computer is instructed to do a job, it handles the task in a very special way. It accepts the information. It stores the information until it is ready to use it. It processes the information. Then it gives out the processed information. People do the same kind of work computers do every day. Let's look at an example.

Mrs. Barker's class has many written assignments. Every day students hand in papers to Mrs. Barker. She puts them into a folder on her desk. At the end of the day, Mrs. Barker corrects the papers. The next day she returns them to her students. Mrs. Barker does the same jobs a computer does.

1. She accepts information.

2. She stores the information.

3. She processes the information.

4. She gives out processed information.

Every computer has a special part to do each of these jobs. All computers, whether they are huge million-dollar mainframe computers or small five-hundred-dollar microcomputers, have these four parts or units: **input, memory, central processing,** and **output.** The following shows how the four parts are related.

The **input unit** accepts information.
The **memory unit** stores the information.
The **central processing unit (CPU)** processes the information.
The **output unit** gives out the processed information.

Processing information
means "doing something
with" the information.

try these

1. Tell the computer job (accept, store, process, give out) and the computer part (input, memory, central processing, output) for each activity in Mrs. Barker's class.

   a. The students give their papers to Mrs. Barker.

   b. Mrs. Barker puts the papers into a folder.

   c. Mrs. Barker grades the papers.

   d. Mrs. Barker returns the graded papers to the students.

2. Here are some activities that go on at Sam's Pizza Parlor. Tell the computer job and the computer part that relate to each activity.

   a. Sam accepts a grocery delivery for the ingredients to make pizza.

b. He has the dough, pizza sauce, cheese, seasonings, and peperoni in bowls on the counter.

c. He shapes the dough into a circle and covers it with the sauce, cheese, seasonings, and peperoni, and bakes the pizza.

d. Sam serves the pizza.

Imagine for a moment! ⇨

If a computer could run the pizza parlor, the *input unit* would accept the grocery order. The *memory* would hold the ingredients. The *central processing unit* would put the ingredients together and bake the pizza. The *output unit* would serve the pizza.

Chapter 3

COMMUNICATING WITH A COMPUTER

Computers are built to do many different tasks. The tasks can be as complicated as controlling a spacecraft in flight or as simple as adding two numbers. Whatever the job may be, a computer must be given a set of instructions in a language it "understands." Let's take a look at how people instruct computers to do tasks.

George pulled up a chair and sat down at his microcomputer. He had heard about the wonderful things computers can do. He was eager to see for himself. He plugged in the computer, turned it on, and waited for something to happen. The computer screen displayed READY, but that's all.

Not all computers display READY when they're turned on. They may print other messages.

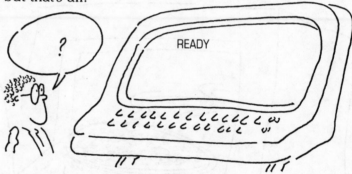

George decided to type this question: HOW MUCH IS 5 + 5? The computer displayed SYNTAX ERROR.

Syntax (sin′taks) refers to the structure of a language. If you type something the computer cannot understand, it displays SYNTAX ERROR.

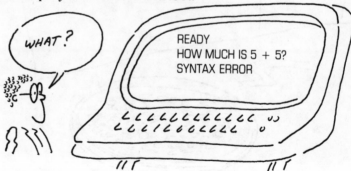

George was puzzled, so he tried something else. Carefully he typed: 5 + 5 = ? Again the computer responded with SYNTAX ERROR.

8

George was having trouble communicating with his computer because he didn't understand how computers work. The computer does not have a "brain" to figure out what George was asking. A computer can't do anything without instructions. A computer is like a car without gasoline. A car won't go anywhere without gas. A computer won't "go anywhere" or do anything without instructions.

A set of instructions that tells the computer what to do is called a **program**. A program might instruct a computer to calculate the balance in a bank account, print out a company payroll, project a flight plan to Paris, quiz a student on pronouns, or play a space monsters game. Programs must be written in a language that the computer can understand. There are many computer languages. Each one is designed for a particular purpose. Some of the common computer languages are:

All computers—mainframe computers, minicomputers, and microcomputers—must have instructions or **programs** to perform tasks.

BASIC	Beginners All-purpose Symbolic Instruction Code
PASCAL	named after Blaise Pascal, 1623-1662
FORTRAN	Formula Translator
COBOL	Common Business Oriented Language
RPG	Report Program Generator

The language used most often in school microcomputers is BASIC. The BASIC language contains ordinary English words, but they must be used in a very precise way. For example, to ask for the sum of 5 + 5 in BASIC, George has to type:

```
PRINT 5 + 5
```

PRINT is a word in the BASIC language.

Then the computer would have displayed the answer 10.

Programs usually consist of many instructions to the computer. The computer "reads" each instruction, and carries it out. Let's take a look at a simple program written in BASIC. It instructs the computer to find the sum and difference of two numbers. When the program is typed into the microcomputer, it will appear on the computer screen this way:

```
1Ø PRINT 192 + 158
2Ø PRINT 192 − 158
3Ø END
```

Most computers put a slash through the number zero so you know it's a zero—not the letter "O".

After each line of the program is typed, it is stored in the computer's memory. However, the computer will not process the program until it is given the command RUN. After RUN is typed, the

RUN is a word in the BASIC language which means "process the instructions."

9

computer will follow the instructions in the program. The computer will "read" the first line of the program (line 10). Then it will calculate and print the sum of 192 and 158, which is 350. The computer will "read" the next line of the program (line 20), and calculate and print the answer to 192-158, which is 34. Then the computer will "read" the next line (line 30), which tells it to stop; there are no more instructions.

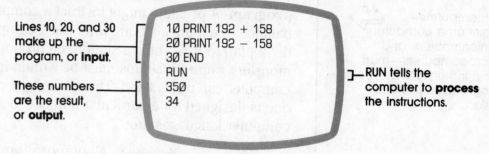

Lines 10, 20, and 30 make up the program, or **input**.

These numbers are the result, or **output**.

```
10 PRINT 192 + 158
20 PRINT 192 − 158
30 END
RUN
350
34
```

RUN tells the computer to **process** the instructions.

Typing and running this computer program involves all four parts of the computer.

Input: The keyboard is used to enter the program into the computer.

Memory: The program is stored in the memory.

Central processing unit: The CPU carries out the instructions in the program.

Output: The video screen displays the results of the program.

There are different ways you can enter a program into a microcomputer. One way is to type in a program yourself. Another way is to use a program that you or someone else has already written and stored on a cassette tape or floppy disk. A tape recorder or disk drive attached to the computer can load the program into the machine. These devices enable you to use the same program over and over again without having to sit down and type in a program every time you want to use it. All computer equipment, such as the keyboard, screen, tape recorder, disk drive, and other attachments to the computer, is called **hardware**.

More about tapes and disks in Chapter 4.

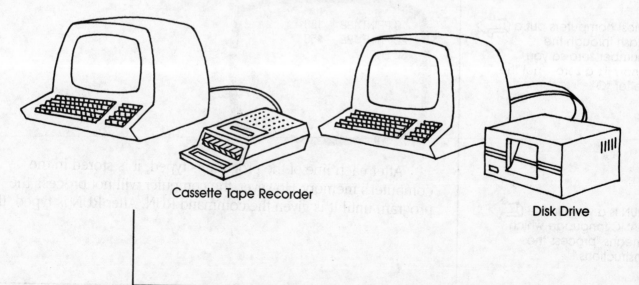

Cassette Tape Recorder

Disk Drive

Computer programs are called **software**. Software that you can buy ranges in price from a few dollars for computer games to thousands of dollars for complicated programs that instruct the computer to do many tasks. Your school may have software for its computers. Some of the software may have been purchased, and some of it may have been written by your classmates or teachers. There are advantages to both buying software and to writing your own programs. Buying software saves a lot of time. It allows you to use a computer even if you don't know how to write programs. Writing your own programs allows you to instruct the computer to do *exactly* what you want it to do.

1. A computer will not work without a set of instructions. What is a set of instructions for a computer called?

2. Name the programming language used for most school microcomputers.

3. What is computer hardware?

4. What is computer software?

5. Name an advantage to buying software for your computer.

6. Name an advantage to writing your own computer programs.

7. Here is an example of a program written in BASIC.

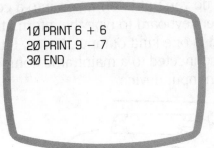

```
1Ø PRINT 6 + 6
2Ø PRINT 9 − 7
3Ø END
```

   a. What is this program instructing the computer to do?

   b. What output will the computer display after following the instructions?

Chapter 4 | INPUT AND OUTPUT

Do you remember the parts of a computer system which accept information and give out the processed information? They are the **input unit** and **output unit**. Let's look at some of the different kinds of input and output devices.

Input Devices

The job of an input device is easy to remember if you break the word into syllables and turn the syllables around.

in-put → put in

When an input device receives its information, its job is to *put* that information *into* the computer.

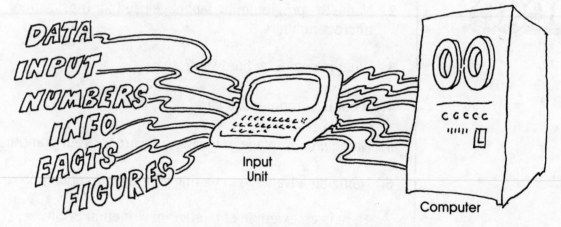

Input Unit

Computer

How do you put information into a computer? One way is to use a computer keyboard to type the information or program. So the **keyboard** is one kind of input device. If the keyboard is part of a terminal connected to a mainframe computer, then the **terminal** is used as an input device.

Some terminals may have a screen.

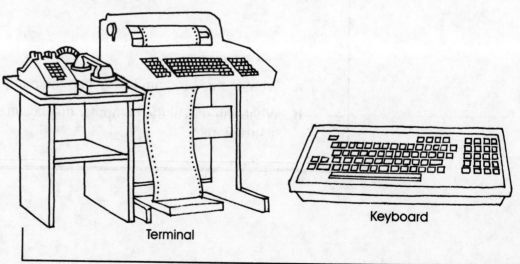

Terminal

Keyboard

12

Many computer programs are stored outside of the computer on storage devices. Programs stored outside the computer can be used over and over again. It takes less time to load a long program into the computer from a storage device than it does to type it in from the keyboard.

There are many kinds of **peripheral input devices** that load programs stored outside the computer. If you have used a microcomputer, you may have used a **cassette tape recorder** as a peripheral input device. **Cassette tape** is a strip of magnetic material. Programs can be stored on ordinary cassette tapes in the form of magnetic impulses recorded on the tape. A tape recorder connected to the computer senses or "reads" the magnetic impulses on the tape. Then it transfers that information into the computer.

Programs for microcomputers can also be stored on **floppy disks,** or **diskettes,** in the form of magnetic impulses. A floppy disk is round (disk-shaped). It looks like a small record, but it bends easily (floppy). Dust or fingerprints can ruin a floppy disk so it is permanently stored in a stiff cardboard holder.

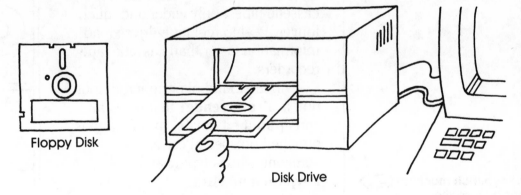

Floppy Disk

Disk Drive

A floppy disk is inserted into an input device called a **disk drive.** The disk drive loads the program into the computer. The floppy disk spins around inside its protective cover like a record spinning on a record player. A **read/write head** in the disk drive glides over the magnetic surface of the disk somewhat like the arm of a record player. Since there are no grooves in a floppy disk, the read/write head does not have a needle. It has metallic pads that read the magnetic impulses on the floppy disk, and load the information represented by those pulses into the computer.

A floppy disk can usually store more programs than a cassette tape. A disk drive loads its information into the computer much faster than a tape recorder. However, a disk drive is much more expensive than a tape recorder.

Minicomputers and mainframe computers often use **hard disk drive units** as input devices. Hard disks are larger than floppy disks, and stiff—not flexible. The surface of a hard disk is magnetic, so hard disks also store information in the form of magnetic impulses. A read/write head in the disk drive senses or reads the information on the disk, and sends it to the computer.

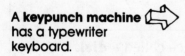
Some microcomputers use hard disks also.

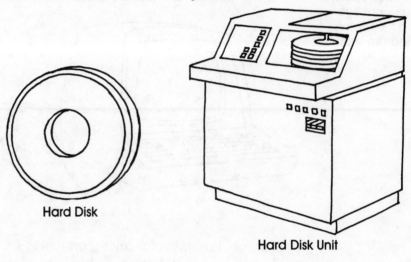

Hard Disk

Hard Disk Unit

Some mainframe computers use **reel-to-reel tape drives** as input devices. Reel-to-reel tapes are like cassette tapes, only wider and much longer. Reel-to-reel tape drives load information faster than cassette tape recorders.

Another kind of peripheral input unit is a **card reader** that reads and sorts **punched cards.** Information is punched on special cards by someone who is typing at a **keypunch machine**. One card is used for each instruction to the computer. Every letter, number, and symbol is shown by a pattern of holes on the card. Here is a card on which the punched holes represent PRINT 1 + 23.

A **keypunch machine** has a typewriter keyboard.

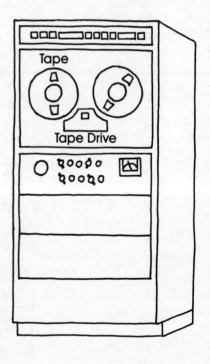

Tape

Tape Drive

```
PRINT  1+23
 ▮ ▮      ▮
0000▮0000000000000000000000000000000000000000000000000000000000000000000000000000
111111▮111111111111111111111111111111111111111111111111111111111111111111111111111
22222222▮2222222222222222222222222222222222222222222222222222222222222222222222222
3333▮3333▮333333333333333333333333333333333333333333333333333333333333333333333333
4444444444444444444444444444444444444444444444444444444444444444444444444444444444
555▮555555555555555555555555555555555555555555555555555555555555555555555555555555
6666666▮666666666666666666666666666666666666666666666666666666666666666666666666666
▮7777777777777777777777777777777777777777777777777777777777777777777777777777777777
8888888888888888888888888888888888888888888888888888888888888888888888888888888888
9▮▮9999▮999999999999999999999999999999999999999999999999999999999999999999999999999
1 2 3 4 5 6 7 8 9 10 11 12 13 14 15 16 17 18 19 20 21 22 23 24 25 26 27 28 29 30 31 32 33 34 35 36 37 38 39 40 41 42 43 44 45 46 47 48 49 50 51 52 53 54 55 56 57 58 59 60 61 62 63 64 65 66 67 68 69 70 71 72 73 74 75 76 77 78 79 80
```

This is one of the oldest methods of *inputting* information. ⇨

Data is information to ⇨ be processed by a computer.

This process is ⇨ sometimes referred to as optical scanning.

The punched cards are placed in the card reader which is attached to the computer. The card reader reads the pattern of holes punched into the cards and sends the information to the computer. Punched cards can be used with micros, minis, and mainframe computers.

An **optical mark reader** is another type of input device. It reads specially marked papers and transfers that **data** into the computer. Optical mark readers are designed to read many papers in rapid succession. For example, have you ever taken a test in which you fill in small circles or lines on an answer sheet? These answers are scored by being run through an optical mark reader. It compares the pattern of marks on the papers to the correct pattern stored in the computer's memory.

Have you ever noticed special "computer" digits on bank checks or bills you receive at home? These digits are printed with magnetic ink. The digits usually show your account number and, on bills, the amount of money that you owe. An input device called a **magnetic ink character recognition (MICR) reader** is able to read the special shape of each digit. It transfers the data to the computer which keeps track of your account.

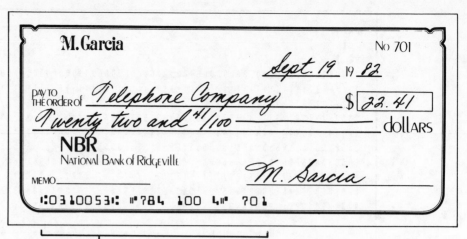

Magnetic Characters

A **light pen** is another type of input device. It looks like a pen and it is connected to the computer by a cable. It senses light on the computer screen and feeds information back to the computer. It can be used to adjust a picture the computer draws on the screen.

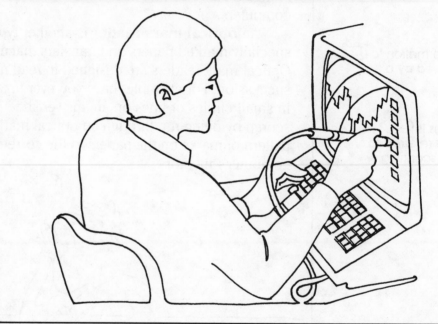

1. What is the job of an input device?

2. Name each device. Some of them are input devices. Some of them are storage devices.

a.

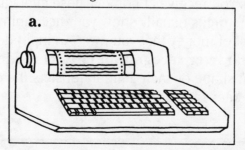

b.

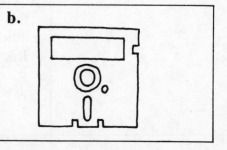

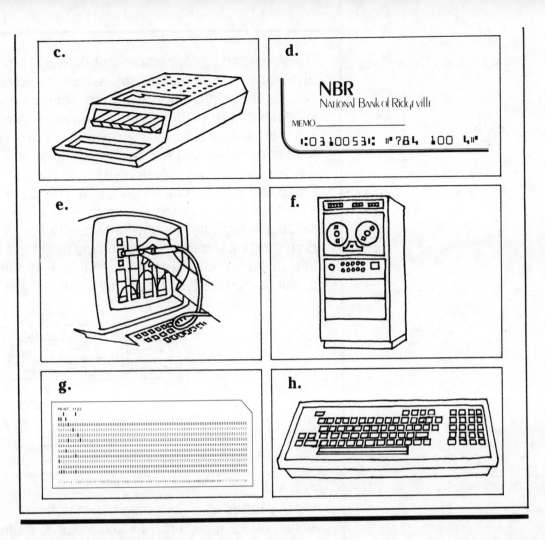

c.

d.

NBR
National Bank of Ridgeville
MEMO _____

1:0310053: "784 100 4"

e.

f.

g.

PRINT 1+23

h.

Output Devices

You can remember what an output device does in the same way you remember input.

out-put → put out

An output device *puts out* the information the computer has processed. There are many ways a computer gives out processed information.

The most common output device on microcomputers and terminals is a **video screen**. The video screen on your computer may be an ordinary television, or it may be a monitor.

A **video screen** looks like a television, but it does not get television channels. Video screens are often called CRTs (cathode ray tubes), or monitors.

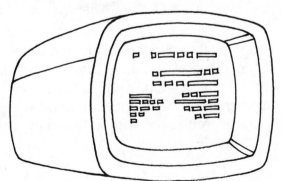

Video Screen or
Cathode Ray Tube (CRT)

A common peripheral output device is a **printer**. Instead of displaying the information on a screen, the computer sends it to a printer. The printer prints the information on paper. Printers vary in speed, but most of them print information faster than you can read it. A printed output is called a **printout** or **hard copy**. A printout or hard copy allows you not only to see the output (as you can see it on a video screen), but also to hold it and carry it around with you. Printouts are important for people who need to refer to their output away from the computer. For example, a salesperson might need a printout of her sales records to take with her when calling on a customer. Or, a credit card company might use printers to print out bills that are sent to customers. In fact, computers wouldn't be as useful as they are if they couldn't produce hard copy.

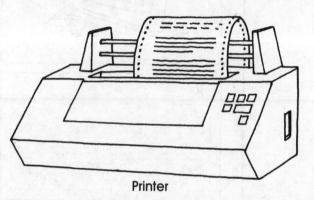

Printer

A **plotter** also gives hard copy output. Instead of printing words and numbers, it plots graphs and pictures. Plotters are very useful to engineers, architects, mathematicians, and other people who use graphs and pictures in their work.

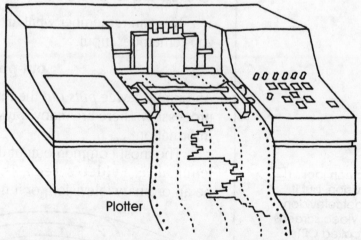

Plotter

Some other peripheral output devices are: cassette tape recorders, floppy disk drives, reel-to-reel tape drives, and hard disk drives. Do these sound familiar? They are also input devices. The computer can *send* information to be stored to these peripheral devices as well as *receive* the stored information from them.

Peripheral devices that do the jobs of both input and output are known as **input/output devices,** or **I/O devices.** For example, you might type a program in your school's microcomputer using the keyboard as your input device. When you RUN your program, you will see the results on the video screen, the output device. You will RUN the program several times and correct any "bugs." Then you will want to save your program on a cassette tape by using a tape recorder, which is a peripheral *output* device. You will give the computer a command to send the information to the cassette tape. Then you can turn off the computer and go home. The next day, perhaps, you will want to show your program to your classmates. Now you will use the cassette tape and recorder as a peripheral *input* device. You type in a command to load the program on the tape into the computer. Then you can run your program. As you can see, the cassette tape recorder has been used as an I/O device.

A **bug** is a programming mistake.

1. Tell whether each unit is an input (I), output (O), or an Input/Output (I/O) device.

a. keyboard

b. cassette tape recorder

c. floppy disk drive

d. reel-to-reel tape drive

e. hard disk drive

f. punched card reader

g. light pen

h. optical mark reader

i. video screen

j. printer

k. plotter

2. Match the type of input device that best fits each situation.

a. A teacher loads a spelling program into a microcomputer.

b. A testing company grades 10,000 answer sheets using a mainframe computer.

c. An engineer adjusts a drawing of an automobile steering system on a computer screen.

d. A student writes a program for a microcomputer.

e. A computer operator loads data on punched cards into a computer.

1. card reader

2. disk drive

3. keyboard

4. optical mark reader

5. light pen

Chapter 5 | MEMORY

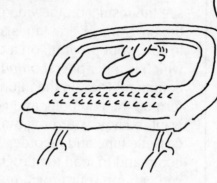

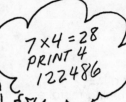

Everyone has a memory. You may be good at remembering some things, and bad at remembering others. Do you remember the names of all the teachers you've ever had? Do you remember the last dessert you ate?

A computer has a memory, too. It's not quite the same as a person's memory. For one thing, a computer's memory can only "remember" or store data, such as facts and figures and programs. It cannot recall the delicious smell of your favorite cake baking in the oven. It cannot remember the wonderful feel of cool water when you jump into a pool on a hot day.

Actually the computer has two kinds of memory. One kind is called **RAM**, or **Random Access Memory**. The other kind is called **ROM**, or **Read Only Memory**. Let's look at RAM first.

Random Access Memory

Random Access Memory, or **RAM**, can be thought of as an empty box, ready to hold information that you type or load into the computer. RAM is the memory where your programs are stored. Unlike your memory, Random Access Memory never forgets the information it is storing, as long as the computer is turned on. To demonstrate RAM's "remembering" power, you could type this short program.

```
10 PRINT "DON'T FORGET ME!"
20 END
```

Remember, data ⇨ means information.

Remember, information can be stored outside of the computer on disks, ⇨ tapes, etc., and loaded into the computer through an input device.

Programs in BASIC can ⇨ be "erased" from RAM by typing NEW.

This program instructs ⇨ the computer to print the words DON'T FORGET ME! on the screen.

20

Some computers have ⇨
keys you can press or
commands you can
type to clear the screen.

Even though the screen ⇨
is blank, the program is
still stored in RAM.

Remember, RUN is the ⇨
command that tells the
computer to follow the
instructions in the
program.

LIST is a word in BASIC. ⇨

Programs that you buy ⇨
are usually protected so
you can't change them.

Then you could clear the screen and leave the computer on.

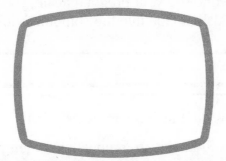

You could come back later in the day, or even the next day, and type in RUN. The computer will demonstrate its remarkable memory. It will recall your instructions and print the output on the screen.

Suppose you want to see the program that is being stored. A program in RAM can be displayed on the screen by typing the command LIST. You can see that the computer has your program stored in RAM.

RAM is a *temporary* memory. This means you can make changes in the information that gets stored in RAM. For example, you can change part of a program or data that is in a program. You can also erase a program and enter a new program into RAM. This allows you to use a computer for many different jobs.

Because RAM is a temporary memory, all the information stored in RAM is lost or erased every time you turn the computer off. This is why we have peripheral input and output devices. If you spent a few hours typing a program on the keyboard, you would not want to turn the computer off. If you did, your program stored in RAM would be lost. Instead, you would save your program on a disk or tape. When you wanted to use your program again, you would load the program from the disk or tape into the computer's RAM.

1. What is the full name for RAM?

2. Why is RAM like an "empty box" when you turn a computer on?

3. Why is RAM called a temporary memory?

Read Only Memory

ROM, or **Read Only Memory**, is the computer's other kind of memory. ROM stores programs that the computer needs in order to operate. Those programs are built into ROM when the computer is assembled at the factory. ROM is a *permanent* memory because its programs are always in the memory, whether the computer is turned on or off. You cannot make changes in the programs in ROM.

Different kinds of computers have different kinds of programs stored in ROM. But most ROMs contain programs that:
put special symbols on the screen, such as the cursor;

Typing NEW does *not* erase the programs in ROM.

10 PRINT "DO■ ——— The cursor is a blinking square or other symbol that shows where the next character will be.

display error messages when necessary;

The command RUN was typed incorrectly, so the computer printed SYNTAX ERROR.

RIN
SYNTAX ERROR

More about this in Chapter 7!

and translate BASIC into the computer's "own" language of binary numbers.

try these

1. What is the full name for ROM?

2. Why is ROM a permanent memory?

3. Give an example of what a program in ROM might do.

RAM and ROM

Computers need both kinds of memory, RAM and ROM, to function properly. ROM stores the permanent instructions to the computer. RAM stores the programs and data you enter into the computer. Below is a review of the computer's two kinds of memory.

RAM Random Access Memory	ROM Read Only Memory
temporary memory	permanent memory
It stores programs you write.	It stores programs built into the memory when the computer is built.
You can make changes in the programs it stores.	You cannot make changes in the programs it stores.

try these

1. Write *RAM* or *ROM* to tell which kind of memory is described.

   a. It stores the programs you write.

   b. It stores programs permanently.

   c. Its programs can be erased or lost.

   d. You can make changes in a program it is storing.

2. How is a computer's memory different from a person's memory?

Chapter 6 | CENTRAL PROCESSING UNIT

CPU

The "brain" of the computer is the **central processing unit**, or **CPU**. It is where all the processing and computing takes place. Even though we call the CPU a "brain," it is not at all like a human brain. It can't think or reason. It can only carry out the instructions it is given. The CPU has two parts—the arithmetic unit and the control unit.

The Arithmetic Unit

The arithmetic unit is the part of a computer system that does the calculations. Even though a computer can be programmed to do very complicated arithmetic problems, the arithmetic unit can only add and compare numbers. If the arithmetic unit can only **add** and **compare** numbers, how can it do other kinds of problems, such as multiplication? Pretend, for a moment, that you can only add—that you never learned to multiply. How would you solve a problem like this?

$$8 \times 6$$

If you remember that multiplication is repeated addition, then you would add:

$$6 + 6 + 6 + 6 + 6 + 6 + 6 + 6$$

Adding eight 6s together might take you a little longer than multiplying 8 and 6, but you could do it.

Why do you think the CPU is referred to as a "brain"? Is it a real brain?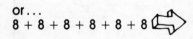

or...
$8 + 8 + 8 + 8 + 8 + 8$

You might even make some mistakes along the way.

The arithmetic unit can also subtract, divide, and do other functions as well. But it does *all* its calculating by changing each problem into an addition problem.

Keep in mind that the computers had to be programmed first so they could solve these kinds of problems.

A computer compares numbers as fast as it calculates.

What if the problem was 34 × 589? If you knew only how to add, not multiply, you would have to add 589 + 589 + 589 + . . . 34 times! You could do that, too, but it would take a *very* long time. A computer does all its multiplication by repeated addition, but it takes the computer practically no time at all. In fact, a computer can calculate this problem in less than a millionth of a second! Even though the computer takes the "long" way of solving a multiplication problem, it is not really long at all.

Scientists measure a computer's speed in nanoseconds. A **nanosecond** is a billionth of a second. It takes about 4 nanoseconds for a computer to solve 25,692 × 587,104,999. This fantastic speed of the arithmetic unit makes the computer a very valuable tool. For example, scientists who plan space flights must solve lengthy problems. If they had to do all the calculations by hand, it would take months, maybe years. But they can use computers to solve the problems quickly, often in minutes or even seconds.

The arithmetic unit is sometimes called the **logic unit**. This is a good name for it since it solves not only arithmetic problems, but also does the "logical" job of comparing numbers. For example, you may have some software for your classroom computer which drills students on math facts. The computer may ask you to type the answer to 4 + 9. The arithmetic or logic unit compares your answer to the correct answer (13), which is part of the program. If the answers are the same, the computer might be instructed to print HOORAY! If they are not the same, the computer might be instructed to print NO, TRY AGAIN.

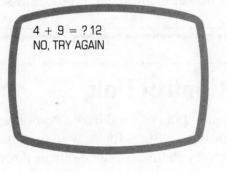

The computer compares this answer to 13.

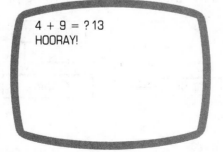

The computer compares this answer to 13.

Another example of the arithmetic/logic unit's ability to compare numbers is when a police officer runs a check for a stolen auto. The officer may call in a car's license plate number to headquarters. The number will be entered into a computer terminal. The computer compares that number to the numbers of license plates from stolen cars that it has stored in its memory. If one of the numbers is a "match", the computer will print out the necessary information for the police.

1. Select the two ways the arithmetic unit processes numbers.

   a. add   c. compare
   b. subtract   d. multiply

2. Why is the arithmetic unit also called the logic unit?

3. Show how the arithmetic unit would solve this problem: 4 × 5.

The Control Unit

When data is entered into a computer through an input device, the control unit directs the flow of that information through the computer. It acts like a police officer directing traffic.

The control unit sends information to the memory to be stored. It also takes the information that is to be processed from the memory.

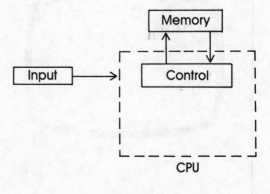

It sends the information to and from the arithmetic/logic unit to be calculated and compared.

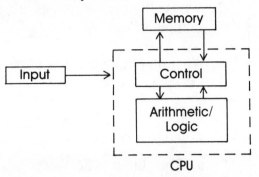

It sends the processed information to an output device to be displayed.

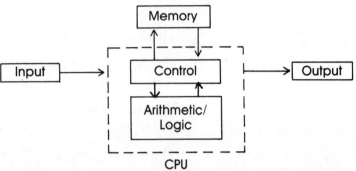

The speed of what other unit is measured in nanoseconds?

As you can see, the control unit is in charge of moving the information to the right places in the computer. It moves the information so quickly, that its speed is measured in nanoseconds. Without a control unit, nothing would move through the computer. There would be a traffic jam!

1. Describe the job of the control unit.

2. Why is the central processing unit called the "brain" of the computer?

3. What unit of measure is used to describe the speed at which a CPU does calculations?

4. A student is doing a spelling lesson on a microcomputer. Tell which part of the CPU, *arithmetic* or *control*, performs each task.

   a. The student's answer is taken from the input unit and put into the memory.

   b. The student's answer is moved from the memory to the arithmetic unit.

   c. The student's answer is compared to the correct answer.

   d. The student's answer is correct, and a "GOOD FOR YOU" message is sent to the output unit.

   e. The answer is incorrect, and a "TRY AGAIN" message is sent to the output unit.

   f. At the end of the spelling lesson, this unit adds up the total number of correct answers.

   g. This unit sends the total number of correct answers to the output unit.

Chapter 7 | CHIPS AND BITS AND BYTES

WHERE ARE RAM, ROM AND THE CPU?

Computer Chips

When you look at a computer, you can see input and output devices such as the keyboard, screen, tape recorder, and disk drive. But where are the memory and the central processing unit? In a mainframe or minicomputer they are usually in a separate piece of hardware that people refer to as the computer. Terminals and other peripheral I/O devices are attached to it. In some microcomputers the memory and CPU are in the keyboard unit under the keyboard. What do the RAM, ROM, and CPU look like? Random Access Memory, Read Only Memory, and the central processing unit are all **computer chips**. What are computer chips and how do they work?

A computer chip looks like a piece of black plastic with metal pins coming out of it. The black plastic is a protective cover around the chip. The pins make it possible to plug the chip into a computer circuit board.

Some chips have a ➾ ceramic (baked clay) cover instead of a plastic one.

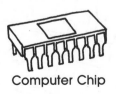

Computer Chip

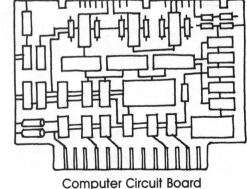

Computer Circuit Board

Silicon (sil′ ə kən) is a common element in the earth's surface found in sand, quartz, and granite. The silicon wafer on a computer chip looks like a thin sliver of metal.

The actual chip is a very thin wafer of **silicon** that measures about one-eighth of an inch on each side. If you looked closely, you might see what appear to be scratches, or etchings, on the metal.

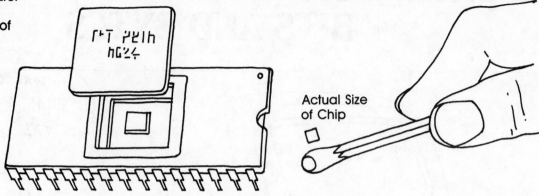

Actual Size of Chip

A circuit (sûr′ kit) is a path through which electricity flows.

If you could look even more closely, you would see that those "etchings" are really very tiny circuits. The circuits weave in and out and around each other. In fact, there are between 10 and 20 thousand circuits on that one tiny chip!

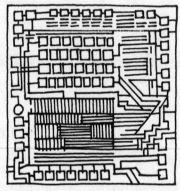

Enlarged Chip

All of these circuits are interconnected, or **integrated** with one another. Therefore, these chips are called **integrated circuit chips**.

How can all these circuits be placed on one tiny chip? The process of putting so many circuits on one tiny chip is called **large scale integration (LSI)**. Large scale integration involves many complex processes. Here are the main steps.

An engineer designs the chip on a computer. A plotter prints out the design.

Remember, a **plotter** is an output device that draws graphs and pictures.

The accurate drawing of the circuits is photographed and reduced to chip size.

The photograph is "baked" onto a thin wafer of silicon. During the "baking" process, the lines on the photograph make an indentation, or etching, on the silicon.

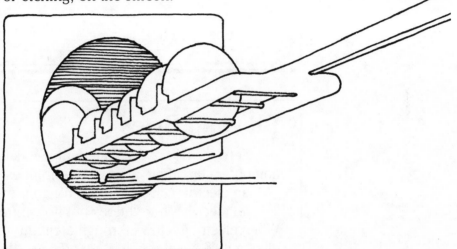

The etched piece of silicon is passed through a magnetic chamber to magnetize the etchings. The magnetized etchings are now capable of conducting electricity—they have become electrical circuits. The chip is then placed in a plastic case with pins. It must be tested and then built into the computer.

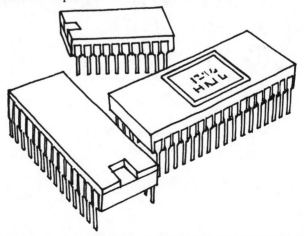

In a microcomputer,  the entire CPU is *one* chip. The chip is called a **microprocessor**.

Most integrated circuit chips cost less than $10.

Of course, not all chips are the same. A ROM chip is different from a RAM chip, and they are each different from a CPU chip. Also, manufacturers make different kinds of ROM, RAM, and CPU chips. The invention of large scale integration has allowed all these kinds of chips to be produced in large quantities at a very low cost. This has led to the development of smaller and less expensive computers that many businesses, schools, and individuals use today.

try these

1. From what element are computer chips made?

2. Approximately how large is a computer chip?

3. About how many circuits are on a chip?

4. What is the full name for a chip with many interconnected circuits?

5. What is the name of the process of putting thousands of circuits on one tiny chip?

Bits and Bytes

Let's see how a computer chip works. For every circuit on a computer chip, there are two possibilities:

an electric current flows through the circuit, or

an electric current does not flow through the circuit.

When electricity flows through a circuit, the circuit is "*on*". When no electricity flows through, it is "*off*." An "on" circuit is also known by the number 1. An "off" circuit is known by the number 0.

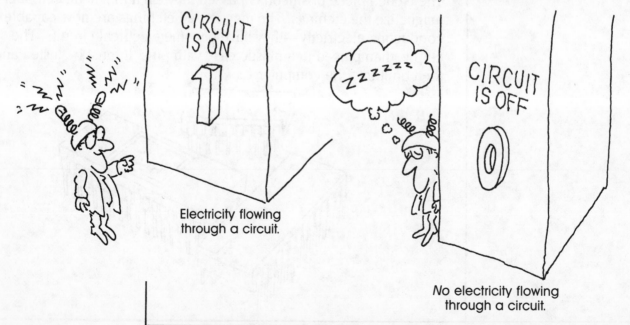

Electricity flowing through a circuit.

No electricity flowing through a circuit.

The prefix **bi** in binary means "two." The binary number system has only two digits, 0 and 1. Our everyday number system is the *decimal number* system. The decimal number system has ten digits, 0 through 9.

The computer uses only the numbers 0 and 1 to do its calculations and processing. These two numbers make up the **binary number system**. The computer needs only the two numbers of the binary number system to do its work because everything it "reads" gets translated into zeros and ones. An instruction read as a 0 instructs the computer to turn a circuit "off." An instruction read as a 1 instructs the computer to turn a circuit "on."

The two digits, 0 and 1, are called **bits**. The word bit comes from binary digit.

binary dig<u>it</u> → <u>bit</u>

Every time the computer "reads" an instruction, it translates that instruction into a series of bits (1s and 0s). In most computers every letter, number, and symbol is translated into *eight* bits, a combination of eight 0s and 1s. For example, when you type the letter A, the computer translates the A into 01000001. The letter B becomes 01000010. Here are some others:

| **X** 01011000 | **Z** 01011010 | **?** 00111111 | **2** 00110010 |
| **Y** 01011001 | **$** 00100100 | **1** 00110001 | **3** 00110011 |

Every single character on the keyboard translates into a different combination of eight bits. These groups of eight bits are called **bytes**. A byte is eight binary digits; that is, eight bits, or eight 0s and 1s.

Byte is pronounced bīt.

0   1   11001101

Bit   Bit   Byte

Let's suppose you type this instruction for your microcomputer.

PRINT "BOO"

The computer translates each character and symbol into a byte (eight binary digits). Each byte tells the computer what to do with its circuits—turn them "on" (electricity flows through) or turn them "off" (no electricity flows through).

| Byte | | Circuits | | | | | | |
		1	2	3	4	5	6	7	8
P	01010000	off	on	off	on	off	off	off	off
R	01010010	off	on	off	on	off	off	on	off
I	01001001	off	on	off	off	on	off	off	on
N	01001110	off	on	off	off	on	on	on	off
T	01010100	off	on	off	on	off	on	off	off
"	00100010	off	off	on	off	off	off	on	off
B	01000010	off	on	off	off	off	off	on	off
O	01001111	off	on	off	off	on	on	on	on
O	01001111	off	on	off	off	on	on	on	on
"	00100010	off	off	on	off	off	off	on	off

The computer continues to translate each character into a byte, and turns circuits "on" or "off" according to the instruction "1" or "0". Even though this may seem like a slow, tedious process, it all takes place in a few nanoseconds of time.

Computer memories are measured in bytes. Your computer's RAM, for example, might be 16,000 bytes. That means your computer can store approximately 16,000 bytes of information. This is 16,000 groups of eight bits, or 16,000 groups of eight circuits turned "on" or "off." Remember, each byte represents one character, such as a letter or number. If you tried to type or load a program that had more than 16,000 characters, the computer would print OUT OF MEMORY.

Another way of referring to the memory size of RAM, such as 16,000 bytes, is **16K** bytes. K stands for *kilo*, or *one thousand*. So 16K stands for 16,000. Microcomputers can have Random Access Memory sizes of 4K, 16K, 32K, 48K, and even 64K bytes. You can buy them with these different memory sizes. You can also add more memory to a computer. If you have a computer that stores 16K bytes, extra RAM chips can be added so it will have a larger memory.

Remember, a 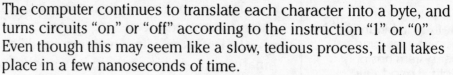 nanosecond is one billionth of a second.

Do you remember what instructs the computer to display this kind of message? A program in ROM does this.

A 16K memory actually stores 16,384 bytes.

Some mainframe computers store 1000K bytes. This is 1000 × 1000 or 1,000,000 bytes!

try these

1. What is the name of the number system used by computers?

2. What do the digits 0 and 1 mean when you refer to the flow of electricity through a circuit on a chip?

3. The *binary digits* 0 and 1 have a shorter name. What is it?

4. When a computer "reads" the character C, it translates it into eight bits (01000011). What is this group of eight bits called?

5. If your computer has a RAM of 16K bytes, what does that mean?

6. If you have a computer in your classroom, find out the size of its random access memory.

CHECKPOINT

Choose the best answer for each.

1. What type of computer system would a major airline use to schedule its flights and make reservations on its flights?

   a. mainframe computer
   b. minicomputer
   c. microcomputer

2. Which of the following is true for a microcomputer?

   a. It can do many jobs at the same time.
   b. It can fit on a desk and can be moved around easily.
   c. It costs over $100,000.

3. Which part of a computer processes information?

   a. input
   b. memory
   c. central processing unit

4. Choose the true statement.

   a. Computers need instructions in order to solve problems.
   b. Computers have brains.
   c. Computers are smarter than humans.

5. Which of the following is a computer language?

   a. English
   b. BASIC
   c. RAM

6. An example of a peripheral input device is a

   a. printer.
   b. punched card reader.
   c. video screen.

7. A computer program is

   a. a computer chip.
   b. a peripheral output device.
   c. a set of instructions that tells a computer what to do.

8. Computer programs are referred to as

   a. software.
   b. hardware.
   c. microprocessors.

9. Which of the following is true about Read Only Memory?

   a. It is a temporary memory.
   b. Its programs can be erased.
   c. Its programs cannot be erased.

10. The arithmetic unit and control unit are parts of

    a. large scale integration.
    b. the central processing unit.
    c. a computer program.

11. The number system used by computers is called the

    a. binary number system.
    b. decimal number system.
    c. metric system.

12. In a microcomputer, RAM, ROM, and the CPU are

    a. input devices.
    b. integrated circuit chips.
    c. binary digits.

UNIT 2
COMPUTERS IN OUR LIVES

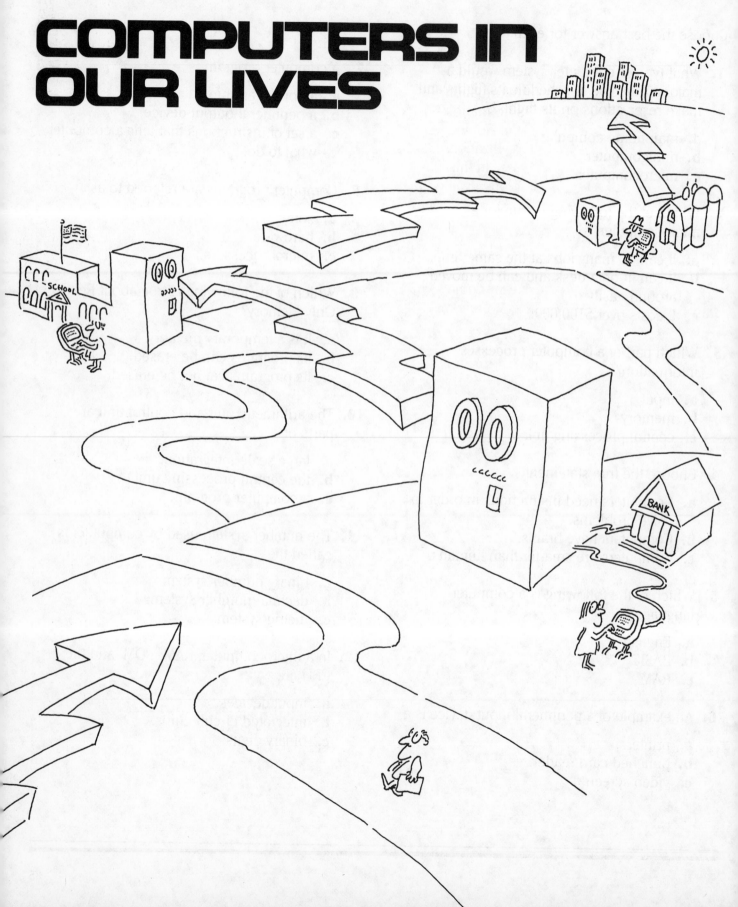

Chapter 8 | FROM ABACUS TO IBM

In Unit 1, you read about what a computer is and how it works. The four jobs of a computer—accepting information, storing information, processing information, and giving out the processed information—are not new ideas. In fact, people have been developing tools to help them do these jobs since the beginning of civilization.

In this chapter, you are going to go back to the past to see some of the developments that led to the invention of modern computers.

Ancient Times

Since the earliest times people used their *fingers* to show "how many." They could show the number of animals killed on a hunt. They could show the number of people living in a dwelling. It was easy to show large numbers in groups of ten by holding up both hands. That is how *ten* became the basis of our number system today.

Primitive people also needed a way to calculate and store information for future use. To keep track of the number of animals killed, they collected small rocks and pebbles in a pile. Each stone stood for one animal. Later they scratched notches and symbols in stone or wood to record and store information.

One of the first tools used to express numbers was the **abacus.** The Chinese abacus was developed about 5000 years ago. It was built out of wood and beads. It could be held and carried around easily. The abacus was so successful that its use spread from China to many other countries. The abacus is still in use in some countries today.

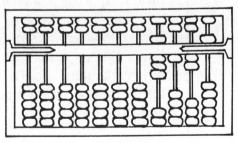
Abacus

The abacus does not actually do the computing, as today's calculators do. It helps people keep track of numbers as they do the computing. People who are good at using an abacus can often do calculations as quickly as a person who is using a calculator!

Numbers are referred to as **digits. Digit** comes from the Latin word *digitus,* which means "finger."

Our number system is called the **decimal** number system. The prefix *deca* means "ten."

The Egyptians, Romans, and Greeks also had versions of the **abacus. Abacus** comes from the Greek word *abax,* which means "board, or calculating table."

The abacus is a storage device. It stores numbers somewhat like the way you use a pencil and paper to store numbers when you compute.

1. What was the earliest method people used for counting?

2. How did this method lead to our use of the decimal number system?

3. What tool, invented by the ancient Chinese, is used to help calculate?

4. Why do you think this ancient device is still used today?

The original rods were made from bone or ivory.

The 1600s

Throughout history, people have developed systems of numbers and ways of counting. They have looked for ways to make calculating easier. In 1617, John Napier, a mathematician from Scotland, invented calculating rods called **Napier's Bones.** The rods were used to help people multiply large numbers.

Napier's Bones

Each rod contained the multiples of a number. By moving the rods around and reading rows of numbers, a person could do a few additions to get the product of two large numbers. The rods did not actually *do* the multiplication. They helped a person compute a product quickly and easily.

Some years later, in 1642, a young French mathematician named **Blaise Pascal** was working in his father's office. His job was to add long columns of tax figures. Doing all this adding was boring and time-consuming. So, Pascal came up with a way to get the job done faster. He invented a machine, the size of a shoe box, that could add and subtract numbers.

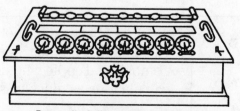

Pascal's Arithmetic Machine

An **odometer** (ō dom' i ter) measures the miles a car travels.

Pascal was only 19 years old when he invented this machine!

Leibniz was also a lawyer and philosopher.

Pascal's **Arithmetic Machine** used gears. They were notched wheels that moved each time a number was added or subtracted. The machine worked very much like an odometer on today's cars. The numbers 0 through 9 were printed on the edges of a row of wheels. When a wheel made a complete turn from 0 through 9, a small notch caused the next wheel to the left to move up one number. The Arithmetic Machine was one of the first machines built that could actually do computing.

During the next fifty years, other calculating machines were invented. They were not much of an improvement over Pascal's Arithmetic Machine. Then, in 1694, a German mathematician, Gottfried Wilhelm von Leibniz, built a very clever calculating machine. It was called the **Stepped Reckoner.** It could multiply and divide as well as add and subtract. Leibniz's Stepped Reckoner used "stepped cylinders" rather than gears and wheels to do its calculations.

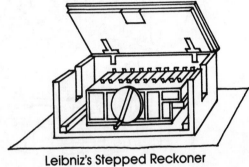

Leibniz's Stepped Reckoner

The machines invented by Pascal and Leibniz were complicated. They had many moving parts. In those days it was hard to build accurate copies of the machines. So, even though the original machines worked well, very few of them were made.

try these

1. Name the inventor of each.

   a. Napier's Bones

   b. Arithmetic Machine

   c. Stepped Reckoner

2. Name the invention that was used to do each of the following.

   a. add, subtract, multiply, and divide numbers

   b. multiply large numbers

   c. add and subtract numbers

3. Why were the Arithmetic Machine and the Stepped Reckoner not widely used?

The 1800s

In 1801, **Joseph Jacquard** of France invented a new type of loom for weaving cloth. **Punched cards** were used to control the operation of the loom. A needle that passed through a hole in the card pulled a thread that became part of the pattern. The threads that could not pass through the card were not part of the pattern at that point. The process was repeated over and over. As a new card moved beneath the needles, its pattern of holes determined which needles would pass through, pulling different colors and kinds of threads. Any time a weaver wanted to repeat a pattern, he simply ran the same cards through the loom in the same order.

Woven fabrics from France were very popular all over the world. French weavers were always looking for faster and better ways to weave their patterns.

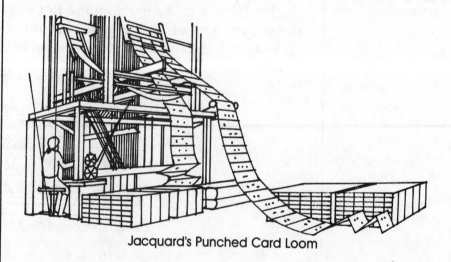

Jacquard's Punched Card Loom

Jacquard did not have computers in mind when he designed his punched-card loom. But, his idea of using punched cards to store information was to be used by a number of computer inventors in later years.

Perhaps the first calculating machine that can be truly called a computer was invented in England by **Charles Babbage** in 1835. Babbage's dream was to build a machine that could do more than calculate big numbers. It would receive instructions. It would process and store information. It would print the results. He planned to call it the **Analytical Engine.** Babbage planned to use punched cards for the numerical information. He also planned to print out the results.

Babbage was a respected scientist, but most people could not understand his new and unusual ideas. He was called "eccentric." He had a hard time finding anyone who would lend him money to build the Analytical Engine. However, a gifted mathematician, **Lady Ada Augusta Lovelace,** saw that the Analytical Engine could be an important machine. She supported Babbage in trying to raise money to build it. One of her most important contributions was to convince Babbage to use the *binary number system* in his machine, instead of the decimal number system. Using binary numbers would make the Analytical Engine work more efficiently.

At first, Babbage wanted to build this machine to compute tables of information for navigation.

Does this sound familiar? These are the four jobs of a computer.

Babbage founded the Analytic Society at Cambridge University in England. Its members spread many new ideas throughout the country.

All computers now use the binary, or base 2, number system. Do you remember what the two digits in this system, 1 and 0, stand for?

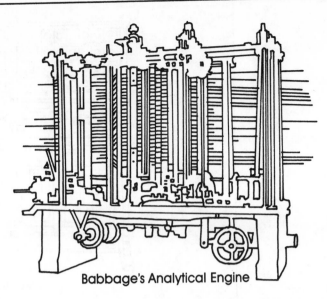
Babbage's Analytical Engine

The U.S. Department of
Defense has its own
programming language
for its computers called
"Ada." The language is
named after Ada
Lovelace.

Ada Augusta Lovelace also wrote about Babbage's plans for the Analytical Engine. From these writings, it is clear that his plans were for those of a modern computer. The Analytical Engine had all four parts of a computer system: input, output, memory, and central processing unit.

Unfortunately, Ada Augusta Lovelace was the only person who appreciated Babbage's plans. Lack of money held up progress. Lack of precision tools made it very hard for Babbage to work on the Analytical Engine. In the early 1800s, electricity was not used. There were only mechanical tools to work with such as gears, cogs, and wheels. The tools of Babbage's time were just not precise enough to build this complicated machine. The Analytical Engine never worked. Babbage died thinking himself a failure. He never knew his ideas would be used more than 100 years later in the first "modern" computer.

A **census** (sen'səs) is a
count of the population.

About fifty years later, another important machine was built. This was **Herman Hollerith's Tabulating Machine.** It was built to help the United States government with the 1890 **census.** The United States government conducts a census every ten years. It collects facts about every person living in the country. So much data was collected in the 1880 census, that by the time it was sorted and tabulated, it was almost time for the 1890 census! An army engineer, Herman Hollerith, found a better way to collect and sort the census data. Hollerith borrowed an idea from the French weaver, Joseph Jacquard—the **punched card.**

Today punched cards
are often called
Hollerith cards.

By this time, electricity
was being used.

Information from each person was punched on cards which were then put through the Tabulating Machine designed by Hollerith. The Tabulating Machine pushed pins against the cards. If a pin went through a hole, it made contact with a metal surface below the card. It completed an electric circuit. This made the Tabulating Machine add one more to the item that was being counted. If there was no hole in the card, no electric circuit was completed. Nothing was added to the total.

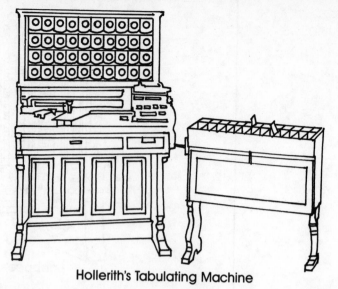

Hollerith's Tabulating Machine

The Tabulating Machine gave a "quick" count of the U.S. population. In fact, it took a little less than three years to tabulate the data for the 1890 census. This was a huge improvement over the 1880 census! The use of the Tabulating Machine was so successful that Hollerith formed a company. It later became known as the International Business Machine Company, or IBM.

Milestones in Computer History			
Year	Invention	Inventor	Country
about 3000 B.C.	Abacus	unknown	China
1617	Napier's Bones	John Napier	Scotland
1642	Arithmetic Machine	Blaise Pascal	France
1694	Stepped Reckoner	Gottfried Leibniz	Germany
1801	Punched Card Loom	Joseph Jacquard	France
1835	Analytical Engine	Charles Babbage	England
1887	Tabulating Machine	Herman Hollerith	United States

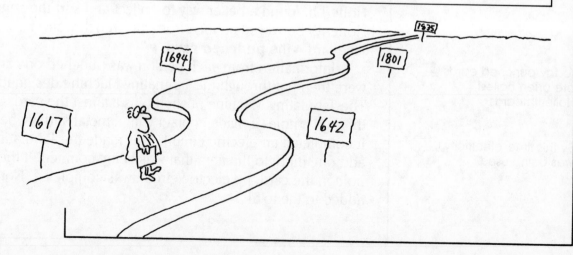

1. Babbage (Analytical Engine) and Hollerith (Tabulating Machine) borrowed an idea for putting information into their machines from the French weaver, Jacquard. What was the idea?

2. For what purpose was the Tabulating Machine designed by Hollerith?

3. How was Babbage's Analytical Engine similar to a modern computer?

4. What important idea did Lady Ada Augusta Lovelace contribute to the Analytical Engine?

5. Some people say that Babbage was "born in the wrong century." Do you agree? Why or why not?

6. Match each description with the correct invention.

   a. used for the U.S. census in 1890

   b. used punched cards to weave patterns in cloth

   c. invented about 5000 years ago

   d. helped people do long multiplication problems only

   e. first machine that was able to add, subtract, multiply, and divide

   f. could add and subtract only

   g. designed to accept, store, process, and give out processed information

   1. Stepped Reckoner
   2. Napier's Bones
   3. Tabulating Machine
   4. Analytical Engine
   5. Arithmetic Machine
   6. Punched Card Loom
   7. Abacus

Chapter 9

FOUR GENERATIONS OF MODERN COMPUTERS

As people learn new things, they use that knowledge to generate more new information. The more information they have, the more they try to find better ways to store it, process it, and retrieve it. During the past forty years, a giant leap has been made in dealing with information. Men and women have developed high-speed computers which accept, store, process, and give out information. The computers work faster than people like Pascal or Hollerith ever dreamed possible.

To **retrieve** (ri trēv′) information means "to get information that is stored somewhere".

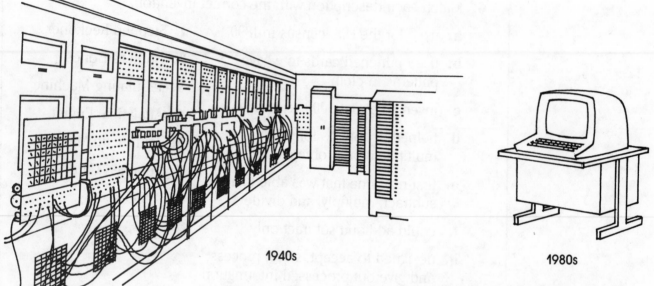

1940s   1980s

The age of "modern computers" began in 1944. In that year an American engineer at Harvard University, **Howard Aiken,** built a computer. It worked very much like a machine designed more than 100 years earlier—Babbage's Analytical Engine. Aiken's computer, called the Mark I, accepted information through punched cards. It stored and processed the information. It printed the results on an electric typewriter. The Mark I was able to do many different tasks. It was a huge machine. It took up the space of a school gymnasium. It took only a few seconds to calculate a math problem—quite a feat for 1944! The Mark I is known today as the world's first **electro-mechanical computer**.

Remember, Babbage was not able to complete his Analytical Engine.

Soon after the invention of the Mark I, scientists began to build computers that had almost no moving parts. That is, they were electronic rather than mechanical. Most of the computers that you'll be reading about are called **digital computers**. A digital computer changes information into digits to be stored and processed.

An **electromechanical computer** has both electrical and mechanical (moving) parts.

Digital (dij′it əl) means "having digits, or numbers."

Electronic digital computers quickly replaced the Mark I. In fact, a few years after the Mark I was built, electromechanical computers became old-fashioned, and weren't used any more.

There have been several major changes in digital computers during the past forty years. Each change ushered in a new "generation" of computers. Just as we have different generations of people in a family, computers have generations, too.

First-Generation Computers

As moving parts inside computers were replaced by electrical circuits, computers worked faster and more efficiently. The first all-digital computer was completed in 1946 at the University of Pennsylvania under the direction of two engineers, **John W. Mauchly** and **J. Presper Eckert.** The computer, called the **ENIAC,** was even bigger than the Mark I. It weighed over 30 tons! It conducted electricity through vacuum tubes. In fact, the computer used over 18,000 vacuum tubes!

The only "movement" in a circuit is the flow of electricity.

ENIAC stands for Electronic Numerical Integrator and Calculator.

Radios and televisions used vacuum tubes through the 1950s.

The ENIAC's electric bill was $1,800 a month in 1946!

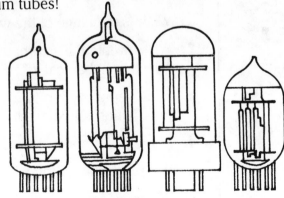

Vacuum Tubes

Vacuum tubes get hot, and 18,000 of them created a lot of heat. So, it was necessary for the ENIAC to have special air conditioning units to keep it cooled down.

The ENIAC was considered quite a "brain." It was 300 times faster than the Mark I. It worked a thousand times faster than a person using a desk calculator. It was given a problem that would have taken 100 engineers, working eight hours a day, an entire year to solve. The ENIAC solved the problem in two hours.

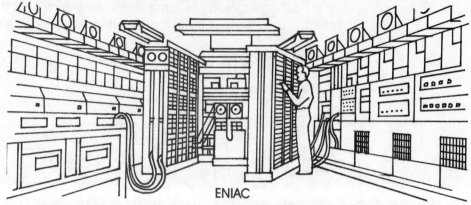

ENIAC

Soon after the ENIAC was built, **John von Neumann** had the idea of storing a computer program in the computer's memory. Up until this time, only the numbers used in the program were stored in the memory. Von Neumann's idea enabled people to build computers that worked faster than the ENIAC. In fact, today's computers are based on von Neumann's idea of storing programs in the memory.

A few years later, in 1951, Eckert and Mauchly designed another computer called the **UNIVAC.** The UNIVAC was even larger than the ENIAC. Eckert and Mauchly sold the UNIVAC to the United States Census Bureau. Other models of the UNIVAC were built and sold, making the UNIVAC the first **commercial** computer. UNIVAC computers are not used today, but the original one can be seen at the Smithsonian Institute in Washington, D.C.

try these

1. What is the name of the world's first electromechanical computer?

2. Who invented this computer? Why is it considered "electromechanical"?

3. What name is given to electronic computers that translate information into digits to store and process?

4. Name two first-generation computers.

5. Who were the inventors of these computers?

6. What devices were used to conduct electricity in the first-generation computers?

7. Pretend you are the president of a large company during the 1950s. Name one advantage and one problem in buying a UNIVAC for your company.

Second-Generation Computers

In the late 1950s, the **transistor** replaced vacuum tubes in the computer. A transistor could conduct electricity more quickly and efficiently than a vacuum tube. It was more reliable, too. Vacuum tubes often "burned out" and needed to be replaced. Transistors rarely needed to be replaced. A transistor was also much smaller than a vacuum tube, and it did not get hot.

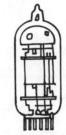

Transistor   Vacuum Tube

When companies started building computers with transistors instead of vacuum tubes, the computers became smaller. They also solved problems ten times faster than first-generation computers.

It is difficult to give credit to any one person for building a second-generation computer. These computers were so complex that it took many people with many different skills to design all the computer parts. Several large companies built these second-generation computers. Some were for their own use. Some were sold to other companies.

One transistor could do the work of about 40 vacuum tubes. It used only about 1/100 of the power. Electric bills for second-generation computers were much lower!

Other improvements included a larger memory and improved input/output devices.

1. What devices were used to conduct electricity in second-generation computers?

2. Name two ways in which this new electrical device was better than vacuum tubes.

3. Why would a company want to purchase a second-generation computer rather than a UNIVAC?

Third-Generation Computers

In 1964, tiny **integrated circuits** were developed to take the place of transistors. These tiny circuits were even faster and more reliable than transistors. Integrated circuits, or IC's, were very small. They took up very little space.

First- and second-generation computers were large machines. They stood on the floor and occupied a lot of space. But the third-

Remember, a circuit is a path through which electricity flows. The path is usually made by a thin wire. "Integrated" circuits are circuits which are connected to each other.

generation computers were much smaller. Some could even sit on top of a table. Also, they could operate 100 times faster than second-generation computers (1000 times faster than first-generation computers!)

Integrated circuits were mass-produced at a low cost. So, as more computers were built with integrated circuits, the price of computers dropped lower and lower. Third-generation computers were inexpensive enough and small enough to be bought by thousands of companies around the world.

Mass-produced means "manufactured in very large quantities."

1. What devices were used to conduct electricity in third-generation computers?

2. What advantage did this device have over transistors?

Fourth-Generation Computers

In the mid-1970s, scientists developed a method of putting thousands of integrated circuits on one tiny silicon chip. The chip itself is so small that it can fit through the eye of a needle. It is difficult to imagine so many circuits on such a tiny surface. It takes many delicate instruments and special scientific techniques to create this "miracle" chip, called an **integrated circuit chip.**

Remember, in Chapter 7 you read that RAM, ROM, and the CPU are **integrated circuit chips.**

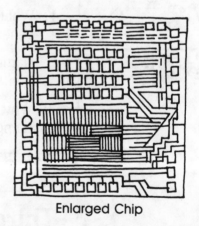

Actual-Size Chip

Enlarged Chip

Integrated circuit chips led to the development of microcomputers.

Integrated circuit chips, or ICCs, are smaller and less expensive than the integrated circuits used in third-generation computers. So, the fourth-generation of computers are even smaller and less expensive than the third-generation computers. Computers built with these chips can perform over 10 million calculations in one second. They are 10 times faster than third-generation computers. (That's 1000 times faster than second-generation computers and 10,000 times faster than first-generation computers!)

1st Generation	2nd Generation	3rd Generation	4th Generation
Vacuum tubes	Transistors	Integrated circuits	Integrated circuit chips
1,000 calculations per second	10,000 calculations per second	1,000,000 calculations per second	10,000,000 calculations per second

As you can see, each generation of computers used a new invention to conduct the electricity through the computer. As the new electrical devices got smaller, the computers got smaller. They became more powerful than the earlier, large computers. They also became less expensive, which enabled small companies, schools, and people to buy their own computers.

try these

1. What device is used to conduct electricity in fourth-generation computers?

2. An integrated circuit chip usually holds how many circuits?
   a. 10 to 20   **b.** millions   **c.** thousands

3. Why are fourth-generation computers used by many companies?

A **voice synthesizer** (sin'thi sīz'ər) produces the sound of a voice.

Future Generations of Computers

What will future generations of computers be like? Computers will respond to a human voice, rather than ordinary input devices such as a keyboard, tape recorder, or disk drive. There are already some computers which can "understand" a small spoken vocabulary. Some computers can "speak" certain sounds through **voice synthesizers**. These output units are being improved so that computers will be able to "talk" and sound almost human.

Scientists are already trying to fit millions of circuits on one chip. That will make computers even smaller and faster than they are now. Small pocket-size computers are already being sold. Some day, computers more powerful than today's will be as common and as small as tiny calculators.

From the time people counted on their fingers to the time the world's first electromechanical computer was built, thousands of years went by. Yet, it took only thirty years from the invention of the big, expensive, and "slow" ENIAC, to the development of small, inexpensive, and fast microcomputers. What caused the rapid changes in those thirty years? New inventions usually open up new areas to explore. They bring about even more new inventions. This has been true with computers. Computers are used to design new computers. When a new and better computer has been built, it can be used to help design an even better computer. What will smaller, more powerful, less expensive computers mean to us? Perhaps, some day, there will be a computer in every home or in every student's school bag!

1. Why are the improvements in computers taking place at a faster and faster rate?

2. Match the electrical device with the computer generation.

   a. integrated circuit   **1.** first generation

   b. vacuum tube   **2.** second generation

   c. integrated circuit chip   **3.** third generation

   d. transistor   **4.** fourth generation

3. As each generation of computers changed, computers became

   a. larger and more expensive.

   b. smaller and less powerful.

   c. smaller and less expensive.

4. If a computer was small enough and inexpensive enough for you to own and carry to school, what would you use it for?

Chapter 10 | COMPUTERS ARE EVERYWHERE

Computers affect our lives every day in many ways. How? Where are they used? Let's take a look.

Computers in Government

The United States government was one of the first computer users. During World War II, the government designed computers to crack the enemy's secret military codes. Today the military forces use computers for tasks such as tracking and guiding aircraft, ocean vessels, and tanks, and for planning defense strategies. They also use computers to keep records of people that are in the military—their rank, jobs, pay, and other important information.

The Census Bureau is a government agency. It uses computers to sort the information it receives every ten years on every person in the United States. The 1980 census had over three billion answers to questions. It would have taken thousands of people more than 10 years to sort all that data. Computers did the job in less than a year.

The Internal Revenue Service is the government agency that collects taxes. Computers keep records of tax forms and check them for errors. Computers print out checks for people who get refunds. Computers also print out notices to people who still owe taxes.

State and local governments also rely on computers to get jobs done. For example, states keep records of all cars, trucks, and other vehicles owned by people. A city might have its traffic lights timed by a computer.

Do you remember when the Census Bureau used Hollerith's punched cards and Tabulating Machine?

There are hundreds of other agencies that use computers for all kinds of jobs.

try these

1. Tell whether or not you think a computer would help to get each job done better.

   a. finding out the number of people who can vote in a state election

   b. choosing a new fire chief

   c. processing paychecks for all the people who work for a city

   d. taking care of the baseball field at the town park

2. How do you think your local police department might use a computer?

Continued

3. One job of the Census Bureau is to give the population of every city, county, and state, in the nation. Match each step of the job with the part of the computer system that does the job.

a. Information is collected and entered into the computer.

b. The information is stored in the computer to be used when necessary.

c. Population figures are added.

d. Population figures are printed out.

1. Memory

2. CPU

3. Input

4. Output

Computers in the Space Program

Spaceships wouldn't get off the ground if it weren't for computers. From the launching of the first spaceship in 1959, computers have been used for space flights. They have helped plan the path of spaceships. They have been used to keep the ships on course and plan their landing.

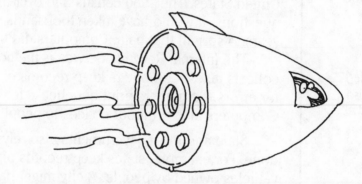

Computers have proved to be very important in emergencies. Several years ago a leak was found in the oxygen tank of the command module of the Apollo 13. There was only a small amount of oxygen left for emergency use. It was important to get the astronauts back to earth as soon as possible. Scientists, programmers, and computer operators at the Manned Spacecraft Center in Houston, Texas, worked non-stop. They gave the computers information to use to plan a new flight path. With each new plan, the computers listed important data. They told how long the return flight would take. They told how much fuel and oxygen would be used. They gave the time and place of the splashdown. Thousands of factors had to be considered. There was not enough time for the control center staff to work out all the calculations by themselves. By using computers, they were able to plan a new course for the Apollo's return. The astronauts were brought safely back to earth.

Computerized equipment found the oxygen leak.

try these

1. Why is it better to use a computer instead of people to do certain jobs when planning a space flight?

   a. The computer knows the correct speeds, path, and landing site without instructions from a human.

   b. The computer can do calculations faster and more accurately.

   c. The computer can tell which day will have the best weather for takeoff.

Computers in Offices

Look at a bill from a department store or a credit company. Was the bill written by a person or printed by a machine? Large companies use computers to keep track of customers' accounts and prepare their bills. It would take many people to do the work of one computer. Computers not only work faster, they are more accurate.

Does that mean that computerized bills never have mistakes? No! Computerized bills cause some very upsetting problems. For example, Mr. Rossi received a bill from a department store for $0.00. So, he ignored the bill. The next month he got a "friendly" reminder (printed by a computer) that he still owed the store $0.00. He wrote a letter to the store asking it to correct the mistake. Before anyone acted on his request, he got another letter (printed by the computer). It told him that if he didn't pay his bill, the store would close his charge account. Before the problem was finally cleared up, Mr. Rossi was very angry—with the computer!

The mistake, of course, was not the computer's fault. In this case it was a programming error. The programmer didn't instruct the computer to stop sending bills when the balance was down to zero. But it was easier for Mr. Rossi to blame the computer.

Computer "mistakes" are not always the fault of the programmer. Sometimes mistakes are made when an office worker accidentally types the wrong information into the computer. Suppose a customer sends a check for $10.50 but the typist enters $1.50. The balance on the next bill will be wrong!

Sometimes the computers themselves cause errors through mechanical or electrical breakdowns. But, these situations are so rare, that "computer errors" are almost always "human errors."

Most large companies use computers to handle many chores. Computers prepare paychecks and keep payroll records. They keep track of inventory and accounts. Computers also process data to give estimates of how much money a company might make at a future date. Why do companies rely so much on computers? Computers can do some work so much faster and more accurately than people. When computers take over boring and tedious tasks, people are free to use their time and skills to reason and make judgments. Computers can do work that requires no thinking, planning, reasoning, or judging 24 hours a day. They can work every day of the year without taking breaks or going on vacation—and they never get tired!

Using computers can save companies money. When that savings results in lower prices to customers, then the computer is helpful to the customer as well as to the company. However, there is a problem in using computers in business. Each new computer often replaces a few office workers. It is a serious problem when a machine takes over a person's job. With all the wonderful things computers do, keep in mind that there are some unhappy results as well.

1. If you were a department store manager, would you want to use a computer to handle these tasks?
   a. Print customers' bills.

   b. Handle a complaint.

   c. Hire a new salesperson.

   d. Keep track of daily sales figures.

2. Suppose you could replace three of your office workers with a new computer. List one benefit and one problem you would consider.

Computers in Supermarkets

When the Thompsons go grocery shopping, they dislike waiting in the checkout lines. Often, there are delays while the cashier looks for the price on each item and rings it up on the register. But, one day, they noticed that the checkout lines were moving very quickly. When it was their turn to check out, they found out why. The cashier did not even look for the prices or ring them up on the register. The cashier passed each item over a "window," called a **scanner,** on the checkout counter. The correct price was automatically printed on the register tape. How did that happen?

The supermarket installed a Universal Product Code computer system. Today, almost all packaged products are marked with a set of black and white bars and numbers. This symbol is called the **Universal Product Code,** or **UPC.**

A **scanner** is an input device in a computer system.

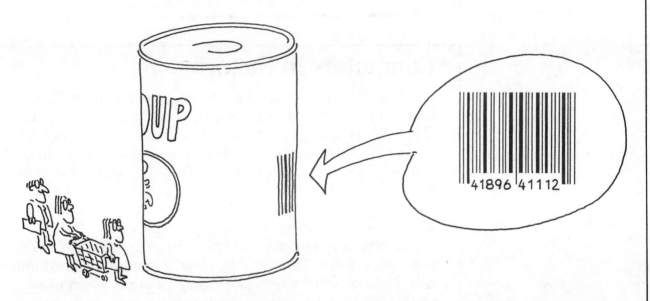

41896 41112

The first few bars and numbers in the UPC usually represent the name of the manufacturer and the product. The remaining bars represent the size of the product.

When the UPC is passed over the bar-code scanner on the checkout counter, the code is "read" by the store's computer. The computer is usually not near the cash register. It might be in an office in another part of the store. It is connected to the cash registers by cables under the floor. The computer translates the code into the product name, size, and price. Then, it sends that data back to the cash register, which prints it on the register tape. The computer also computes the tax, if any, on each item. All this happens in less than a second. This is faster than having the cashier ring up each price. When all the items have been entered, the computer calculates the total bill. It sends the total to the cash register in less than a second. Using the UPC system makes the checkout time go much faster.

Universal Product Codes save the supermarkets a lot of time, too. Since the packaged products already have a code on them, the store clerks do not have to stamp prices on every item. Some stores post prices on the shelves. A UPC system also keeps better track of the store's inventory. Each time the computer reads a UPC code, the records stored in its memory are changed. They show one fewer item remaining in the store. This is much faster and more accurate than counting items left on the shelves at the end of the day.

The memory and CPU are in the computer.

The cash register tape is the output.

Some customers miss having the prices marked on individual items.

55

1. How would a Universal Product Code computer system help a supermarket? Name two ways.

2. What benefits might customers get from a UPC system in a supermarket?

3. Name something a customer might not like about a store's UPC system.

Computers in Factories

At a steel mill, an arm reaches into a blast furnace. The temperature is over 1000 degrees. The arm removes a red-hot metal object. Who could get so close to that intense heat? No person could get that close. But a robot's steel "arm" is able to. Robots do many dangerous jobs in factories. They work in very hot or cold or polluted environments. Robots are also used for tasks that must be done over and over again. This allows factory workers to spend more time on jobs that require human skills and intelligence.

A robot is a computer that has been programmed to do certain tasks. Some robots are "arms" with many "fingers" that perform delicate tasks. Other robots look like large boxes which move around. They deliver machine parts to stations along their computerized routes. Robots neither look nor act like humans. But there will be more and more of them working next to people in factories.

1. Why is it a good idea to use robots for some jobs in factories?

2. Which jobs are more suitable for a robot than a person?

   a. punching holes in metal sheets
   b. checking for damaged furniture in a furniture factory
   c. dipping metal rods into acid solutions

Computers in Banks

The Spencer family decides to go to a movie on a Sunday. They don't have enough cash at home and the banks are closed. That isn't a problem. On the way to the show, they stop at the bank. Mrs. Spencer inserts a plastic bank card in the 24-hour automatic teller. She punches in her bank code and pushes a button to get cash. The automatic teller gives her the money. All across the country, banks are installing computerized automatic tellers. They allow customers to withdraw cash, make deposits, and pay bills any time of the day or night.

An automatic teller has a special keyboard.

A **deposit** is money put into an account.

Banks also use computers to keep track of checking and savings accounts. In Chapter 4, you read that bank checks have account numbers printed on them in magnetic ink. An input device called a Magnetic Ink Character Reader reads the numbers on the check.

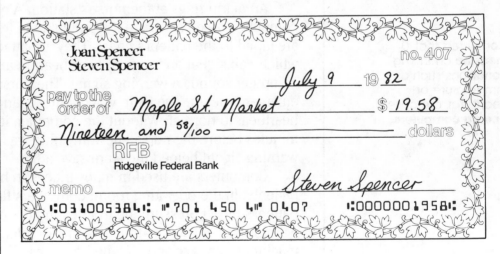

When the bank cashes this check, a clerk types the amount in the lower right hand corner. These are magnetic characters also. The banks computer "reads" the Spencers' account number and the total. It subtracts $19.58 from their account. Each month, the computer prints a list of checks cashed, deposits made, and the balance. This list, or *statement,* is mailed to the Spencers.

The **balance** is the total amount left in the account.

Banks use computers for many other things, too. They compute interest on loans and savings accounts. They keep track of how much money a bank is able to lend. They also compute how much money a bank may have at a given moment. There is so much activity in a bank that it would be impossible to keep records without computers.

1. Suppose you are a bank president. Which of these jobs would you use a computer for?
   a. Hire a new manager.

   b. List all the loans made to customers.

   c. Keep all checking account records.

   d. Explain what a special savings account is to a customer.

2. How might a 24-hour automatic teller be good for a bank's customers?

Computers in Hospitals

An alarm rings at the nurse's station. A quick look at the computer screen shows that a patient is in trouble. Electronic sensors are taped to the patient's chest. They are attached to a computer which can signal an irregular heartbeat. In a split second, the computer sounds a warning signal. The nurse summons an emergency team. The team works quickly and restores the patient's heartbeat to normal. Without the computer, it could have been several minutes before the nurse knew anything was wrong. The computer warning signal helped the team save a life.

Computers are used in many places in hospitals to monitor patients. In the operating room, computers flash information about a patient's blood pressure, heart rate, and temperature on a screen. A warning signal sounds if there is any problem. Computerized X-ray machines can take very detailed pictures. They allow doctors to see things that would not show up on ordinary X-rays. Computers also help interpret the results of laboratory tests.

Computers help the hospital staff gather information and interpret results. Will computers ever take over the roles of doctors, nurses, and other hospital personnel? No. Human judgment will always be necessary and desirable when treating people.

1. Name one way in which computers are used in hospitals.

2. Why won't computers ever replace doctors and nurses?

Remember, a **terminal** is an input/output unit attached to a mainframe or minicomputer.

A **word processing** program instructs the computer to process, or manipulate, words.

Computers in Newspapers

Not long ago, newspaper reporters sat at their typewriters, typing their stories. They would often tear up the pages and start over again until everything was "just right." Today, many newspaper rooms are no longer filled with the sound of clacking typewriter keys. Instead, reporters use computer terminals. As they type on silent keyboards, their stories appear on video screens. They use a computer program that does **word processing.** With word processing, a reporter never has to throw away a page or cross out a mistake. Instead, a few keystrokes instruct the computer to take out certain words (or sentences, or paragraphs), insert others, and move sentences around—right on the screen.

When the story is ready, the reporter types an instruction to store it in the newspaper's main computer. When all the stories are ready, the computer prints out each one. The stories fit neatly in columns!

Newspapers aren't the only places that use word processing. Companies that do a lot of writing and typing use word processing. For example, a company might send out thousands of letters to announce a new product, sale, or contest. The letters have a "personal touch." They begin with "Dear Mr. Birnbaum" (or your name). Someone typed the letter only once! The letters are not written and typed one at a time. They are prepared by a computer using word processing.

The computer inserts the individual names from a list of data it is storing.

try these

1. Name one way in which using word processing is better than using a typewriter.

2. Do you think people enjoy getting computer-written "personal" letters? Why or why not?

Computers in Schools

It's time for social studies. Joanne is working on map skills. She gets to the classroom computer and loads a program. An outline map of the United States that shows major rivers appears on the screen. The computer prints a question under the map: WHAT RIVER MARKS THE BOUNDARY BETWEEN THE UNITED STATES AND MEXICO? Joanne looks at the map and types in RIO GRANDE. The computer responds with RIGHT, JOANNE! Then it asks another question. Mountain ranges, states, and major cities appear and disappear on the screen as needed.

Is this a special school or a classroom of the future? No. Many classrooms have computers which can help students in many subjects. Using computers to help students learn is called **Computer Assisted Instruction,** or **CAI.**

Why use a computer? A computer is very patient. It will not yawn or get bored, upset, or angry if you take a long time to answer a question. Also, when you type in your answer, the computer will tell you immediately if it is correct or not. No waiting until the next day to get your score.

However, a computer can't take over the role of a teacher. It doesn't explain things in different ways. You can't ask it *any* question. Also, it has no feelings. It won't sympathize with you if you've been home for a week with the flu. A computer is a very precise machine. Your answer must be exactly right, or the computer will count it wrong. And, of course, a computer can't give you a real smile or a pat on the back.

Computer Assisted Instruction is sometimes referred to as Computer Based Education.

Suppose you typed RIO GRAN instead of RIO GRANDE. Your teacher might know what you mean, but the computer won't.

Computers are also used to teach programming skills, such as those in Unit 3 of this book. There may be computers in your school that do other things. A computer in the office might store student records and keep track of attendance. It might also print out class schedules and report cards.

try these

1. What does CAI stand for? What does it mean?

2. Which of these exercises do you think a student could do on a computer in the classroom?

   a. Identify subjects and verbs.

   b. Observe how sunlight and darkness affect plants.

   c. Practice multiplication facts.

   d. Create a clay sculpture.

   e. Memorize a poem.

   f. Name the capitals of states.

Computers in Your Home

Some people have computers in their homes. They may use them to keep family records such as taxes and bank accounts. They may use them to store records such as important dates or recipes. Many people use their home computers to play games or to learn how to write programs.

Some day computers might be as common as televisions in homes. They will be used to store information such as phone numbers, addresses, appointments, and bank accounts. They will probably be connected to mainframe computers outside the home. This will let people communicate with stores, banks, and news services. For example, you would be able to look at a store catalog on the screen. Then, you could order items by using your keyboard. To pay for the items, you would transfer money from your bank account to the store's account. You would do all of this at home, using your computer.

Is there a computer in your house? Think, for a moment, what a computer is. It's a machine that can accept, store, process, and give out information. Remember, the memory stores information. The central processing unit processes the information. The memory and CPU are **integrated circuit chips.** Do you think you have any of

Remember, integrated circuit chips are smaller than your fingernail.

61

these chips in your house? You probably do. Do you have a digital clock or watch? An electronic game? A microwave oven with a "memory"? A new color television? A new car? A sewing machine that can be programmed? A push-button telephone? A calculator? All of these items contain computer chips. They usually have a memory chip and a CPU chip. The input units are the buttons, dials, and switches you use to operate these appliances. The output units are display screens such as the numbers on your digital watch. They are also electronic signals such as the telephone connection you make with your friend in another city.

You probably do have some of these computers in your home. The difference between these computers and "personal" or microcomputers is that the computers in your home are built into other appliances. They are designed to perform specific tasks rather than a wide variety of tasks. Now ask yourself again, is there a computer in your home?

1. Name two things that people use microcomputers for at home.

2. Name three items in your home that probably have integrated circuit chips in them.

Computers Play Many Roles

You have read about computers in many areas of your everyday life. If this book covered every way computers are used, it would be too big and too heavy to carry! If you look around, you will probably become more aware of the roles computers play in other things you do.

Many of the tasks computers are used for fall into four categories: **information retrieval, data processing, process control** and **simulation.**

Information retrieval means retrieving or getting back information that has been stored. You can think of the computer as a "dictionary." You can use it to look up what you need to know. For example, the Census Bureau keeps computerized records. When employees need certain data, they use the computer to get, or retrieve, information. A store manager uses a computer to check the inventory. The computer is being used for information retrieval.

Data processing means taking data, that has been input, and doing something with it. For example, a bank's computer is used for data processing when it keeps track of your bank account. A computer in a company is used for data processing when it computes bills, payrolls, and sales reports.

Process control means using the computer to control certain situations. For instance, a computer in a steel factory is used to regulate the temperature of a furnace. It controls that particular process of making steel. A computer which regulates the flow of gasoline to a car engine is used for process control.

Simulation means imitating a particular real-life situation on the computer. Computer simulations are used to plan space flights, for example. A simulation might show the path and speed of a spaceship, as if it were really in flight. A person using the simulation could change the speed of the ship and see what would happen to the flight plans. Running a simulation on a computer helps spot possible problems before they really happen.

Astronauts also ⇨ practice certain procedures during **simulated** space flights.

1. Here are some computer uses. Tell whether each one is an example of information retrieval, data processing, process control, or simulation. Some may have more than one answer.

   a. The Internal Revenue Service keeps track of the taxes people owe.

   b. The commander of an army regiment gets a printout of all the people in the regiment and their ranks.

   c. A computer on board a spacecraft controls the flow of oxygen in the spacecraft.

   d. A department store prepares a monthly bill for each customer.

   e. A supermarket's UPC checkout system keeps inventory records.

   f. An automatic bank teller gives out money and prints out the customer's new balance.

   g. A computer regulates a patient's breathing machine in a hospital operating room.

   h. Newspaper reporters type their stories on a word processor.

   i. You use your school computer to pretend you are a pioneer in the 1700s. You must face many problems as you cross the country.

   j. Your television set automatically adjusts the color and sharpness of the picture.

   k. Your family plays an electronic television game together.

Chapter 11

OTHER COMPUTER USES—AND MISUSES

Remember, many ➪ computer files are storage devices such as tapes and disks.

You have seen how computers can help people in government, businesses, homes, and other places. Computers store and process large amounts of information very quickly. This ability makes computers important tools. But it also poses some problems. What kind of information should be kept in computer files? What happens if secret or personal information gets into the wrong hands? In this chapter, you will see some of the ways that computers can be misused. You will look at what steps have been taken to correct these situations.

Computers and Privacy

Remember, **interest** is the extra charge paid on a loan. ➪

A **credit check** helps ➪ determine whether a person is able to pay back a loan.

Mr. and Mrs. Green want to buy a car from the Economy Car Company. They want to buy it on credit. That is, they will pay part of the price when they get the car. They will pay the rest with monthly payments, plus an interest charge.

But first, the Economy Car Company wants to run a credit check on the Greens. The company wants to know if the Greens are able to make the payments. To get the answer to that question, the Economy Car Company turns to a **credit bureau.** Credit bureaus collect information, or data, about people. Then, they sell the data to companies that want to check a person's credit. If the data shows that the Greens are a good "risk", then the Economy Car Company will sell them a car on credit.

Data held by credit bureaus is in the **data banks.** Data banks are collections of computer files—tapes, disks, or punched cards that can be read by computers in a few seconds. It is easy for credit bureaus to collect, store, and retrieve huge amounts of information. This data includes many details about every person in their files.

Much of the information held in data banks is personal information. The Greens' file might show where they live and what jobs they have. It might show whether they own or rent a house and how much money they have borrowed. It might show if they have served in the military, if they have been arrested, or if they have ever been sued.

Do computers "know" too much? Some people think so. Of course, computers do not "know" anything. But, they store personal information. There is a concern that information might be given to people who aren't supposed to have it. Suppose a neighbor found out information about the Greens from a credit bureau. That would be an invasion of the Greens' privacy.

Laws have been passed to protect privacy. Credit bureaus can collect only data which affects your credit rating. They must keep this information private. They can sell it only to companies or agencies that have a right to know that information. So, a credit bureau is not allowed to give out information about the Greens to a neighbor.

Another concern is that data banks may contain wrong information. For example, when the Kaplans bought a new couch for their home, it arrived damaged. They refused to pay the store for the couch. The store sued the Kaplans for the money. A judge ruled that they did not have to pay. The Kaplans won the case. Or did they? The credit bureau's data bank showed that the Kaplans did not pay the bill. They were listed as being a poor credit risk.

You have the right to know what is in your files. If you find a mistake, and the credit bureau agrees, the mistake will be corrected. If the bureau does not agree, you can have the bureau include your side of the story in your file. So, the Kaplans were able to correct their file.

Another concern is how to deal with information from many years past. Suppose a family did not pay their bills several years ago. Should a poor credit rating stay in their files forever? A poor credit rating could make it impossible for them ever to get a loan or buy on credit.

Bankruptcy means "being unable to pay money you owe."

Information about unpaid bills and bankruptcy must be destroyed after seven years. That way, someone who has been a poor credit risk can start over again with a "clean slate."

Credit bureaus are not the only places that have data banks. Many businesses store data about the people they serve. Insurance companies keep records about their clients. Hospitals keep records about their patients. Probably the largest collection of data banks belongs to the United States government. Data banks are owned by the armed forces, FBI, Internal Revenue Service, Immigration Service, and hundreds of other government agencies. The government needs to have information in order to provide services for its citizens. For example, the Internal Revenue Service must know how much money each person earns in order to collect the fair amount of income tax. The FBI needs to learn as much as possible about criminals it is after. The Immigration Office must check applications to be sure they do not allow people to enter the country illegally.

Computerized data banks help government agencies do their jobs more efficiently. But, many people worry that agencies have so much private information about people. What if the information was misused or used against someone?

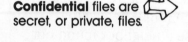
Confidential files are secret, or private, files.

Privacy laws also apply to government agencies. All files are confidential. An agency is not allowed to give information to anyone without a sound reason, unless you give written permission. Agencies that collect personal data must tell what kinds of files they are keeping. In many cases, you can look at your files, and correct them if necessary.

Computers have made it possible to collect, store, and process millions of facts about millions of people. It is up to you and all citizens to be sure that data banks are used for the benefit of people. They should never be used against people unfairly.

try these

1. A bank is usually thought of as a place that stores money. What do data banks store?

2. Which facts do you think the Economy Car Company has a right to know before selling a car to the Greens on credit?

   a. how much money Mr. and Mrs. Green earn

   b. where they live

c. how much money they give to charity

d. whether they owe other companies money

e. how the Greens get along with their neighbors

3. Which facts do you think a government agency should get from a data bank before hiring a new worker?

a. whether the person is a U.S. citizen

b. whether the person has friends

c. where the person has worked before

d. how much money the person has in the bank

Computers and Crime

Every day more computers are bought by businesses, governments, and people. Also, more and more people are becoming highly skilled in using computers. This growing use of computers has led to another type of problem. It is as new to society as computers themselves—computer crime. What is computer crime? It's not stealing a computer. It's usually using a computer to carry out an illegal act. This type of crime might involve stealing money, property, or information through the use of a computer.

For example, a computer crime took place a few years ago when a California bank was robbed of over 10 million dollars. How was so much money stolen? Who were the robbers? Did they carry weapons? How did they get away?

There was only one robber. He carried out the crime alone. He did not set foot near the bank vault! He was a computer specialist who was hired to work on the bank's computers. He was able to find the computer that was used for transferring money to other banks. He found out the secret code which tells the computer to transfer money from that bank to other banks. He used it to transfer over 10 million dollars to a bank account he had set up in another country.

The bank did not know right away that the money had been taken. Banks transfer billions of dollars every day. At first, bank officials thought this transfer was part of the daily business. But within five days of the crime, the robber was caught and the money was returned.

In another example of computer crime, a bank teller used his terminal to transfer small amounts of money from his customers' accounts to his own account. He, too, was eventually caught and punished.

Any place that uses
computers could be a
target.

Banks are not the only targets for computer criminals.
Companies designing new products have had their plans stolen.
Sometimes computer tapes or disks are stolen. But stealing plans
right out of the computer's memory is more common. Some computer
criminals are people who have access to a terminal. They find out
how to tie in to a company's mainframe or minicomputer. Then they
get information illegally. Some computer criminals do not steal
information. They change it. This causes many problems for the
people who need to use that information.

How can computerized information be protected? In large
computer systems, safety devices such as passwords and number
codes are used. They can be programmed into the system. If
someone tries to use the computer without entering the correct
password, the computer may "lock up." It might even be programmed
to "call" a security guard by setting off a buzzer.

Passwords and codes do not always provide enough security to
protect important information. Sometimes passwords and codes are
stolen. Sometimes computer criminals have broken the codes. These
are problems that everyone has to deal with. Companies and people
who use computers must protect their private information as much as
possible. Computer designers must continue to find better ways to
protect computer systems. All of us must see that laws are passed
and enforced to protect information and punish computer criminals.

1. Do you think a computer can be blamed for a computer crime?
   Why or why not?

2. In what way do you think computer crime could cause a serious
   problem for you?

Chapter 12 | COMPUTER CAREERS

Computers play a role in everyone's life. Computers affect us in some way every day. Some people have decided to be more involved with computers. They have chosen computer careers. There are many kinds of jobs that deal with computers. Some jobs involve working with computer software. Some involve working with computer hardware. Let's take a look at some computer jobs.

Careers with Computer Software

Programmer   You know that a computer can't do anything without instructions. A programmer writes the instructions, or program, to tell the computer how to do a particular job. Programmers must know the language of the computer they are writing instructions for. Remember, computers are designed to "understand" certain languages such as BASIC, Fortran, COBOL, and others. Most programmers know several computer languages. This allows them to write instructions for many different kinds of computers.

Many programmers are college graduates who have studied computer science. Some jobs require a programmer to have some special knowledge of a subject area. For example, a programmer who instructs a computer to design a bridge needs some engineering background. Someone who writes a program to simulate a chemistry experiment needs a science background. Some programmers who work for large companies also have a business background.

Keypunch Operator   Programs, along with a lot of data, must get into the computer somehow. In large companies, programs and data are usually typed in by a keypunch operator. A keypunch operator does not have to know much about computers. In fact, a keypunch operator may never even see a computer while working. A keypunch operator uses a keypunch machine with punched cards or a terminal with a keyboard and a video screen.

For example, a large department store uses a mainframe computer to handle all its billing. Each time a customer pays a bill, that data is entered into the computer by a keypunch operator.

Keypunch operators are usually high school graduates. They do not need any special knowledge about computers. But they do need to be good typists. If a keypunch operator makes a typing mistake, someone's bill will be wrong!

Software Librarian   Some companies have hundreds or even thousands of programs and data files. They are kept on tapes, disks, or punched cards. When a program or data file is needed, it must be

Remember, **software** refers to computer programs; **hardware** refers to the computer machinery.

The data might be a series of names or numbers.

found quickly. So tapes, disks, and cards are stored in software libraries which are run by software librarians. A software library has a filing system for storing each piece of software, just as a library has a system for storing each book. Software librarians are usually high school graduates who are good at organizing and record-keeping.

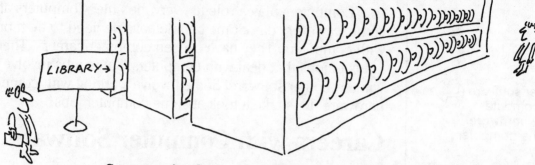

Systems Analyst How does a company go about computerizing its record-keeping or other jobs? There needs to be a great deal of planning before a computer is even bought. A systems analyst works with a company to develop an overall plan to use computers in the business. A systems analyst must study the jobs to be done. He or she must decide how a computer could do them more efficiently. (In some cases, the systems analyst might decide that using a computer is *not* the best way to handle a certain job.)

After the systems analyst has made a thorough study of the company, several suggestions will be made. The plans will tell what kind of computer (or computers) to buy; where they should be located; what jobs they will do; and what kinds of programs need to be written. The systems analyst will instruct the programmers as to what tasks their programs should accomplish.

Systems analysts are college graduates. They usually have graduate training. They must have a good background in business and computer science.

Careers with Computer Hardware

Computer Engineer You know that the most important parts of a computer are the integrated circuit chips. Although the chips are tiny, they contain thousands of circuits. Each one must be put in the right place. It must be connected to other circuits in exactly the right way. Designing this pattern of circuits is the job of a computer engineer. Computer engineers try to improve chips by designing new patterns of circuits. They often use computers to help them develop the new patterns.

Computer engineers also design entire computer systems. They design the input and output devices. They plan how the memory and central processing unit chips will connect to the input and output devices. They must be sure that all the computer parts work together. A flaw in one small part of the computer can cause the entire system to stop working.

Graduate training involves going to college beyond the usual four years.

Computer engineers must have a good background in electrical engineering. Their training usually includes a college degree and often a graduate degree as well.

Computer Technician   When computer parts are designed, they must be tested, put together, and tested again by a computer technician. Sometimes technicians do drafting work. Drafting is making drawings from plans prepared by an engineer. Some technicians are known as service engineers or field technicians. These are people responsible for maintenance and repair work on computers. Computer technicians usually have technical training from a technical school, two-year college, or the armed forces.

Computer Operator   Computer operators are the people who actually run the computers. If you have operated a microcomputer in your classroom, then you have an idea of a computer operator's job on a small scale. Computer operators are hired to run mainframe computers. They attach tapes or disks to input devices which load programs into the computer. They put punched cards into card readers to load programs and data. They also operate printers when hard copy output is required.

Remember, **hard copy** is the output printed on paper.

Computer operators are usually high school graduates. Some computer operators receive their computer training in a technical school. Also, many companies include on-the-job training for their computer operators.

Other Computer-Related Careers

Sales Representative   Computer systems are sold by sales representatives. They serve as a link between computer manufacturers and the people who use computers. Salespeople have to know how their computers work. They also have to understand their customers' businesses well enough to explain how a computer can work for them.

Sales representatives work closely with design engineers and programmers to keep up-to-date with the computers they are selling. Computer salespeople must not only have a good technical background. They must get along well with other people.

Many salespeople have a college degree.

Public Relations and Advertising   People involved in explaining their company's products to the public are in public relations and advertising. This area is especially important for computer companies. It is the job of public relations and advertising people to explain about computers in a manner that is easy to understand. It is their job to advertise in a way that makes people want to buy their computers.

Artists and writers work in public relations and advertising departments. Good clear writing and accurate precise drawings help to explain computers to the general public.

Technical Writers   Every new computer that is sold is accompanied by manuals—books that explain how to work the computer. Some manuals also explain how to program the computer. People who write these manuals are technical writers. They are usually college graduates with a strong electronics background and good writing skills.

Computer Teachers   A lot of companies use computers for many tasks. Their employees must be taught how to use computers. Sometimes sales representatives or public relations people train employees. But often, computer teachers are hired to handle this task. Computer teachers must have a strong background in computer technology. They must also be familiar with a company's business so they can explain how to use the computers.

Many schools are also hiring computer teachers. They are people who have acquired computer skills in addition to their other teaching skills. They teach computer literacy, data processing, or programming in different computer languages to their students.

1. Some computer careers involve working closely with a computer. Others involve working more closely with people. (Of course, all jobs involve working with people to some extent.) Tell whether each career emphasizes working with computers or working with people.

   a. programmer

   b. keypunch operator

   c. software librarian

   d. systems analyst

   e. computer engineer

   f. computer technician

   g. computer operator

   h. sales representative

   i. public relations and advertising

   j. technical writer

   k. computer teacher

2. Which job or jobs are most appealing to you? Why?

CHECKPOINT

Choose the best answer for each.

1. What is the ancient Chinese device that helped people calculate?

   a. Abacus
   b. Stepped Reckoner
   c. Tabulating Machine

2. In 1835, Babbage designed a machine that could accept, store, process, and give out information. Name the machine.

   a. Napier's Bones
   b. Analytical Engine
   c. Punched Card Loom

3. When were computers first made to be sold to companies?

   a. 1950s
   b. 1900s
   c. 1840s

4. What devices conduct electricity in today's fourth-generation computers?

   a. vacuum tubes
   b. transistors
   c. integrated circuit chips

5. Which job would *not* be suitable for a computer in a department store?

   a. Calculate customers' bills.
   b. Process paychecks.
   c. Handle customers' complaints.

6. Using a computer to keep track of customers' checking accounts is an example of

   a. simulation.
   b. data processing.
   c. process control.

7. Using a computer to control the temperature in a building is an example of

   a. process control.
   b. simulation.
   c. information retrieval.

8. If your computerized bill has an error, it was probably a

   a. mistake made by a computer.
   b. mistake made by a person.
   c. poor electrical connection.

9. One concern people have about data banks that contain personal information is

   a. how fast data is processed.
   b. computer breakdowns.
   c. individual privacy.

10. Computers can be blamed for crimes.

    a. true
    b. false
    c. sometimes

11. A person who writes computer programs is a

    a. keypunch operator.
    b. computer operator.
    c. programmer.

12. A person who services and repairs computers is a

    a. sales representative.
    b. computer technician.
    c. software librarian.

UNIT 3
BASIC PROGRAMMING

Chapter 13 | MEET YOUR COMPUTER KEYBOARD

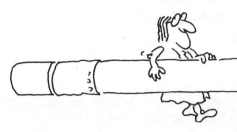

At Your Desk

In this unit, each chapter has two parts—"At Your Desk" and "At the Computer." "At Your Desk" introduces you to words and symbols in the BASIC language. It shows you how to use them when you write programs. When you get to "At the Computer," take this book with you and work the exercises on a microcomputer.

Now it's time to start communicating with your computer. First, let's take a look at the input device you will be using—the keyboard.

This is a TRS-80 keyboard. If you don't have a TRS-80 computer, your keyboard will have some differences.

Some micros have a number "keypad" on the right side of the keyboard.

Atari computers do not slash the zero.

If you have used a typewriter, you will see that a computer keyboard is similar to a typewriter keyboard. The keys are not in alphabetical order. On the keyboard above, find these letters:

A P B S T I N

Did you notice that the letters are all upper-case (capital) letters? Most computers use only upper-case letters.

The number keys are on the top row of the keyboard. Look at the number zero. It has a slash through it. This helps you tell the difference between the number zero and the letter O.

Some keys have special symbols on the top. For example, the number 4 (on the top row) has a dollar sign ($) above it. To type a

Look at the keyboard 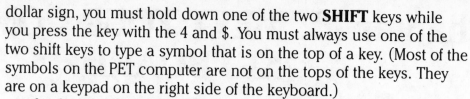 picture. Find the SHIFT keys and the key with 4 and $.

dollar sign, you must hold down one of the two **SHIFT** keys while you press the key with the 4 and $. You must always use one of the two shift keys to type a symbol that is on the top of a key. (Most of the symbols on the PET computer are not on the tops of the keys. They are on a keypad on the right side of the keyboard.)

Look at the keyboard and find the **space bar**. It is a long bar below the bottom row of keys. Every time you press the space bar, the computer prints a blank space on the screen.

I AM A COMPUTER.

The spaces between the words are "printed" by pressing the space bar.

The Apple, Atari, and PET computers have a RETURN key.

There is a special key on the keyboard that you will be using a lot. On the TRS-80 computer it is the **ENTER** key. On some other computer keyboards it is the **RETURN** key. This key "enters" the instructions of your program into the computer's Random Access Memory (RAM). You must press this key each time you finish typing an instruction.

As you use your computer keyboard more and more, you will have an easier time finding the keys and knowing how to use them. Let's see how much you already know about the keyboard.

Choose the correct answer.

1. Which of these is the number zero?

  a. O
  b. Ø

2. The letters on the keyboard are

  a. upper-case letters.
  b. lower-case letters.

3. To send an instruction to the computer's memory, you must press

  a. ENTER (or RETURN).
  b. SHIFT.

4. Look at the picture of the keyboard. Tell whether or not you have to use the SHIFT key to type these symbols. Write *yes* or *no*.

  a. !   **e.** ?
  b. =   **f.** .
  c. %   **g.** ,
  d. −   **h.** +

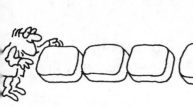

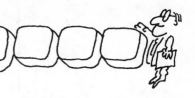

At the Computer

Some computers do not have a **prompt**.

Cursor comes from the Latin word *cursor*, which means "runner." The cursor "runs" across the screen.

Some computers have a] for a prompt. Some have a ___ for a cursor.

It's time to use your microcomputer. You'll be typing some of the things you just learned about. Be sure your computer is plugged in and turned on. Look for the on-off switch behind or under the keyboard. The on-off switch is hard to reach—on purpose! If you accidentally turn off the computer while typing your program, you'll lose everything in the Random Access Memory. RAM is where your program gets stored.

Be sure that your computer is ready to be used—that is, a **prompt** and **cursor** should be on the screen. The **prompt** is a symbol that means the computer is waiting for you. The **cursor** shows where the next character will appear on the screen as you type. The prompt and cursor are different symbols on different microcomputers. Here is a sample of a prompt and a cursor.

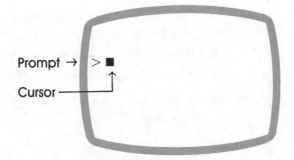

Now you are ready to type. Use both hands when you type. It may seem hard at first. But, with practice, it will be easy to find the keys you want. Also, using both hands will help you type faster.

Using the Keyboard

1. Type your name on the screen. Press the space bar to put a space between your first name and last name. Watch the cursor move as you type.

2. Now erase your name.

   If you have an Apple computer, move the cursor back to the beginning of your name by pressing the left-facing arrow (←). Then press return.

   If you have an Atari computer, move the cursor back by pressing the BACKS key. The letters will disappear as you move the cursor.

If you have a PET computer, move the cursor back by pressing the DEL key.

If you have a TRS-80 computer, move the cursor back by pressing the left-facing arrow (←). The letters disappear as you move the cursor.

3. Find these characters on the keyboard and type them:

   `A 2 0 Ø , . / ; -`

4. Now press the ENTER (or RETURN) key. This tells the computer to enter the information you typed into its RAM. The computer displays an error message. The error is a **syntax error**. The message will either be the words ERROR, SYNTAX ERROR, or an abbreviation such as SN ERROR. The computer did not understand your instruction when you entered it into RAM, so it gave you an error message. It is as though the computer is saying, "I don't understand you!" The reason that the computer did not understand you is because you did not type an instruction in the BASIC language. That's OK for now. The computer will ignore those characters and wait for another instruction.

Syntax (sin' taks) refers to the structure of language.

5. Now practice typing some other characters even though the computer will not understand what you are typing. Find the keys that have symbols on the top. Press the SHIFT key and type the symbols on the tops of those keys.

6. Press the ENTER (or RETURN) key again. You will get a syntax error message! The computer did not understand you.

7. Now clear the screen.

   If you have an Apple computer, press the ESC key, then type the symbol @. (You have to hold down the SHIFT key to type @.) You can also type HOME to clear the screen.

   If you have an Atari computer, press CLEAR. (You need to hold down the SHIFT key.) You can also type GR.0.

   If you have a PET computer, press CLR. (You need to hold down the SHIFT key.)

   If you have a TRS-80 computer, press the CLEAR key *or* type CLS.

Writing in BASIC

1. This time, let's write something the computer will understand—a message in BASIC. Type this line:

   `PRINT "HELLO"`

Remember, BASIC is a computer language.

78

Then press ENTER (or RETURN). The computer will display:

```
PRINT "HELLO"
HELLO
```

PRINT is a word in the BASIC language. The computer understands it. The computer will *print* whatever is in the quotation marks.

2. What if you forget the space between PRINT and HELLO? It doesn't matter. The computer ignores all spaces except those inside the quotes. Try typing this. Don't leave any spaces:

    ```
    PRINT"HELLO"
    ```

    Press ENTER (or RETURN) after you type this.

    You will see the same result as before. Spaces are used to make instructions easier for *people* to read.

3. What if you misspell the word in quotes? The computer prints whatever is in quotes. It will follow your instructions exactly as you type them. Try typing:

    ```
    PRINT "CMPUTER"
    ```

    Press ENTER (or RETURN) after you type this.

    The computer will print:

    ```
    CMPUTER
    ```

4. What if you misspell the word PRINT? Try typing:

    ```
    PRONT "HELLO"
    ```

    Type PRONT instead of PRINT.

    You will receive an error message. When you misspell a word in BASIC, the computer cannot understand your instruction. Any mistake in a computer instruction is called a **bug**. You will see this "Bug Alert" reminder throughout this unit to help you avoid common errors.

5. If you have entered an instruction with a bug, type it over again. Retype the instruction:

    ```
    PRINT "HELLO"
    ```

    This time, retype it without the bug. Then, enter it.

6. Now clear the screen and type this instruction:

    ```
    PRINT "SO LONG"
    ```

    If you are not sure how to clear the screen, look at page 78.

    Look back at page 77.

    If you see a mistake before you enter the instruction, you can erase the line by backing up to your mistake and typing the rest of the line again. If you see a bug after you have pressed ENTER (or RETURN), you cannot get back to that line. Retype the line instead.

Chapter 14 | SAY HELLO TO YOUR COMPUTER

At Your Desk

You might have seen a computer print messages or answers to problems on the screen.

HELLO! WHAT'S
YOUR NAME?

HOW MUCH IS
324 + 678?

THE TEST RESULTS ARE:

STEVEN   95%
JOANNE   98%
SPENCER   87%

You know the computer does not have a brain. It could not have printed these messages unless it was instructed to do so. A set of instructions that tell a computer what to do is a program.

How are programs written? How do you know what to tell a computer? First, you need to decide what you want the computer to do—solve a problem, print a message, or do some other task. Next, you work out a step-by-step plan, or **algorithm**, that the computer is to follow. Then, you write each step in a computer language. (You'll be using the BASIC language.) This set of steps, written in a computer language, is your program.

In this chapter, you will learn how to instruct, or program, a computer to print messages and to do arithmetic problems. You will also use punctuation marks to have the computer display results in different ways.

Using PRINT Statements

Look at this program.

```
10 PRINT "I LIKE COMPUTERS"
20 PRINT "COMPUTERS LIKE KIDS"
30 END
```

What do you think the program will instruct the computer to do? It's not a mystery. If you guessed that it will instruct the computer to print I LIKE COMPUTERS and COMPUTERS LIKE KIDS on the screen, you are right.

Let's look at how the program was written. Each instruction starts with a **line number**. The lines must be numbered in the order you want the computer to follow them, starting with the lowest number. Let's follow the program the way the computer does. This is called **tracing** the program.

You may use any ⇨ numbers for your line numbers, but programmers usually skip 10 lines at a time.

Line 10 contains the word PRINT and words inside quotation marks. PRINT is a statement in BASIC. It instructs the computer to *print* whatever is inside the quotation marks—words, numbers, symbols, and spaces. Line 10 tells the computer to print I LIKE COMPUTERS.

Line 20 tells the computer to print COMPUTERS LIKE KIDS.

Line 30 is the statement END. END lets the computer know it has reached the *end* of the program.

When the program is typed, it is stored in the computer's Random Access Memory, or RAM. The computer won't follow the instructions in the program until you tell it to. How do you get the computer to follow your instructions? You type the command RUN. RUN tells the computer to follow the instructions stored in RAM. Here is what the screen looks like now.

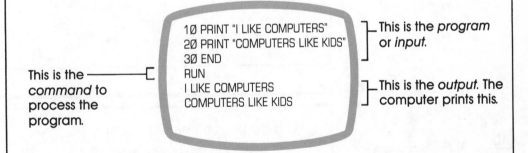

This is the ——— command to process the program.

```
10 PRINT "I LIKE COMPUTERS"
20 PRINT "COMPUTERS LIKE KIDS"
30 END
RUN
I LIKE COMPUTERS
COMPUTERS LIKE KIDS
```

⌐ This is the *program* or *input.*

⌐ This is the *output.* The computer prints this.

RUN is a **command**. It tells the computer to do something immediately. It is not part of the program. It does not have a line number. PRINT and END are **statements**. They have line numbers. They get stored in RAM. The computer does not follow the instructions in lines with line numbers and statements until it comes to the command RUN.

The output is what the computer displays on the screen below RUN. The output is the result of the instructions you typed in the program. Look carefully at the output and notice that the computer printed only the words and spaces inside the quotes. It did not print the line numbers. It did not print the word PRINT. It did not print the quotes. But, it did print the results on two separate lines—the way they were set up in the program. Why didn't the computer print END?

Because the END statement simply tells the computer it has reached the end of the program.

Here is a program that instructs the computer to print a picture of a rocket ship made up of symbols and spaces.

```
10 PRINT "   *   "
20 PRINT "  ***  "
30 PRINT " ***** "
40 PRINT " *   * "
50 PRINT " *   * "
60 PRINT " *   * "
70 PRINT " ***** "
80 PRINT " !!!!! "
90 PRINT " !!!!! "
```

Here is what you see when you RUN the program!

```
RUN
     *
    ***
   *****
   *   *
   *   *
   *   *
   *****
   !!!!!
   !!!!!
```

The computer printed the stars, exclamation points, and spaces that were inside the quotes.

1. Here is a computer program.

```
10 PRINT "DO YOU SPEAK ENGLISH?"
20 PRINT "I SPEAK BASIC!"
30 END
```

a. Trace the program—that is, explain what each line is telling the computer to do.

b. What would the output of this program be?

2. Write the output for this program.

```
10 PRINT "HELLO, COMPUTER"
20 PRINT "* *I AM FINE* *"
30 PRINT "GOODBYE!!"
40 END
```

Don't forget line numbers, PRINT, quotes, and END.

Remember the rocket ship?

3. Write a program that will give this output.

NO SCHOOL TODAY . . .
IT'S SATURDAY

4. Design your own picture using PRINT statements. You can use as many lines as you need.

Calculating

Look at the program and output on this screen. The computer printed the "message" in the quotation marks.

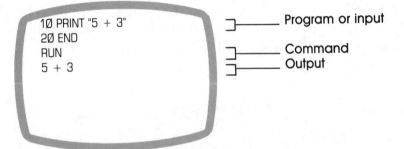

```
10 PRINT "5 + 3"
20 END
RUN
5 + 3
```

Program or input

Command
Output

Now look at this program and output.

```
10 PRINT 5 + 3
20 END
RUN
8
```

WHAT HAPPENED? THIS OUTPUT IS DIFFERENT!

Do you see the difference between line 10 in this program and line 10 in the program above it? In this program, there are *no* quotes in the PRINT statement. PRINT 5 + 3 instructs the computer to calculate the answer to 5 + 3, and print *only* the answer—8.

This program tells the computer to subtract two numbers. The output is the answer to 10 − 4, which is 6.

```
10 PRINT 10 − 4
20 END
RUN
6
```

WHAT AN EXPENSIVE CALCULATOR!

This program shows some more calculating.

```
10 PRINT 3 * 4
20 PRINT 16/2
30 END
RUN
12
8
```

What do you think the symbols * and / mean? The star (*) is the symbol for multiplication. 3 * 4 means 3 times 4. You cannot use × for multiplication because it represents the *letter* X. The slash (/) is the symbol for division. 16/2 means 16 ÷ 2. There is no division sign on the keyboard, so the slash is used for dividing.

Now look at this program. It combines two things you know about PRINT statements.

```
10 PRINT "7 + 5 ="
20 PRINT 7 + 5
30 END
RUN
7 + 5 =
12
```

Line 10 tells the computer to print whatever is in quotes. So the computer prints 7 + 5 =.

Line 20 does not have quotes. It tells the computer to calculate and print the answer to 7 + 5, which is 12.

Line 30 ends the program.

Did you notice that the ⇨ slash makes the division problem look like a fraction? That's because fractions are a form of division.

One PRINT statement ⇨ has quotes, and one doesn't.

Let's *trace* the ⇨ program.

1. Write the output for this program.

```
10 PRINT 12 + 3
20 PRINT 9 − 1
30 PRINT 6 * 2
40 PRINT 8/4
50 END
```

2. Write the output for this program.

```
10 PRINT "24/6 ="
20 PRINT 24/6
30 PRINT "3 * 3 ="
40 PRINT 3 * 3
50 END
```

3. Write a program that will give this output.

```
15 − 4 =
11
```

4. Write a program that will give this output.

```
THE ANSWER IS
10
```

You decide which numbers and operation you want to use.

Using Punctuation Marks

You already know the output of this program.

```
10 PRINT "26 + 5 ="
20 PRINT 26 + 5
30 END
RUN
26 + 5 =
31
```

Now look at what a **semicolon (;)** at the end of line 10 does to the output.

```
10 PRINT "26 + 5 =";
20 PRINT 26 + 5
30 END
RUN
26 + 5 =31
```

The semicolon tells the computer to *continue the output on the same line,* not to go on to the next line.

Combining instructions saves time. You don't have to type a new line.

You can also use the semicolon to put more than one PRINT instruction on a line with just one PRINT statement. Let's trace this program.

```
10 PRINT "12 * 3 =";12 * 3
20 END
RUN
12 * 3 =36
```

Line 10 could have been written this way:

```
10 PRINT "12 * 3 =";
15 PRINT 12 * 3
```

The semicolon separates the part of the line in quotes from the part of the line *not* in quotes. The semicolon also instructs the computer to continue the output on the same line.

Line 20 ends the program.

Remember, a semicolon (;) in a PRINT statement tells the computer to *continue on the same line.*

Look at the program below. It uses **commas (,)** in the first three PRINT statements. Look at the output. The four answers are on one line, and they are separated.

```
10 PRINT 12 + 8,
20 PRINT 16 − 4,
30 PRINT 8 * 5,
40 PRINT 20/4
50 END
RUN
20    12    40    5
```
⊐——Output from lines 10, 20, 30, and 40

Imagine that the computer screen is divided into four sections called **zones.** A comma in a PRINT statement tells the computer to *continue its output in the next zone.*

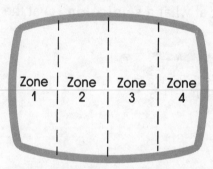

| Zone 1 | Zone 2 | Zone 3 | Zone 4 |

A comma can also be used to put more than one PRINT instruction on a line with just one PRINT statement.

```
10 PRINT 15 + 5, 15 − 5, 15 * 5
20 PRINT 12 + 3, 12 − 3, 12 * 3
RUN
20        10        75
15         9        36
```
⊐——Output from line 10
⊐——Output from line 20

Perhaps you have seen computer printouts with many figures listed in columns. Often a PRINT statement with commas is used to print output in neat columns.

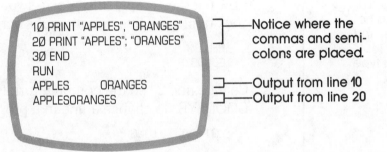

```
                    SCHOOL ENROLLMENT
                                        NUMBER OF
          TEACHER        HOMEROOM       STUDENTS

          R. JACOBS        122            28
          S. CONWAY        123            26
          R. RODRIGUEZ     124            27
          J. FRITZ         125            22
```

Commas and semicolons can be used in PRINT statements in the same program. Whether you use a comma, a semicolon, or no punctuation depends on what you want the program to do and on what you want the output to look like. Remember, a comma is used to combine instructions and print output in different zones on the same line. A semicolon is also used to combine instructions, but it makes the printed output run together on the same line. Look at the output of this program.

```
10 PRINT "APPLES", "ORANGES"
20 PRINT "APPLES"; "ORANGES"
30 END
RUN
APPLES        ORANGES
APPLESORANGES
```

— Notice where the commas and semi-colons are placed.

— Output from line 10
— Output from line 20

try these

When you write the answers, leave spaces to show zones.

There's more than one way to write this program.

1. Write the output for this program.

   ```
   10 PRINT "18/3 =";
   20 PRINT 18/3
   30 END
   ```

2. Write the output for this program.

   ```
   10 PRINT 1 * 1, 2 * 2, 3 * 3
   20 END
   ```

3. Write the output.

   ```
   10 PRINT "COMPUTERS", "ARE", "FUN"
   20 PRINT "COMPUTERS"; "ARE"; "EASY!"
   30 END
   ```

4. Write a program that will give this output in zones.

   ```
   HA      HA      HA
   ```

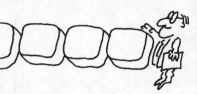

At the Computer

In this section, you will practice writing programs at the computer. You will be using the PRINT statement and punctuation marks in PRINT statements. But, first, you will learn how to make changes in programs by changing lines, adding lines, and taking out lines.

Making Changes

1. Type this program carefully.

   Remember to press ENTER (or RETURN) when you finish typing each line.

   ```
   10 PRINT "HELLO"
   20 PRINT "GOODBYE"
   30 END
   ```

   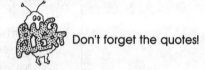 Don't forget the quotes!

   Now tell the computer to process your program by typing RUN. You should see this output on the screen:

   ```
   HELLO
   GOODBYE
   ```

   Remember RUN is a command. It does not get a line number. You must press ENTER (or RETURN) after you type RUN.

2. Change line 20 so the computer prints SO LONG instead of GOODBYE. To change a line in a program, just retype the line:

   ```
   20 PRINT "SO LONG"
   ```

   Type this.

   Your screen should look like this.

   ```
   10 PRINT "HELLO"
   20 PRINT "GOODBYE"
   30 END
   RUN
   HELLO
   GOODBYE
   20 PRINT "SO LONG"
   ```

3. Now type the command LIST. LIST tells the computer to display the program stored in RAM. Notice that your "new" line 20 has replaced the "old" line 20.

   Since LIST is a command, it does not get a line number.

   ```
   LIST
   10 PRINT "HELLO"
   20 PRINT "SO LONG"
   30 END
   ```

4. Now run your program by typing the command RUN. This time your output should be:

   ```
   HELLO
   SO LONG
   ```

5. Clear the computer screen.

   If you have an Apple computer, press ESC, then press SHIFT and @. You can also type HOME.

   If you have an Atari computer, press CLEAR *or* type GR.0.

   If you have a PET computer, press CLEAR.

   If you have a TRS-80 computer, press CLEAR *or* type CLS.

   Did you lose your program? No, it's still stored in RAM. You simply cleared the screen, not the computer's memory. Display your program again by typing LIST.

6. Add another line to your program so that the output will have I'M A COMPUTER between HELLO and SO LONG. To add a line to your program, choose a line number between 10 and 20 and type the line you want. Here's an example:

   ```
   15 PRINT "I'M A COMPUTER"
   ```

7. Now display the program in RAM by typing LIST. See how the computer has inserted line 15 in the right order. Your program should look like this:

   ```
   LIST
   10 PRINT "HELLO"
   15 PRINT "I'M A COMPUTER"
   20 PRINT "SO LONG"
   30 END
   ```

   Now run the program.

8. Take out the line that prints HELLO. To do this, type the number of the line you want to take out:

   ```
   10
   ```

   Is the line still there? It's on the screen, but it is no longer in the computer's memory. Type LIST to see the program stored in RAM. You should see:

   ```
   LIST
   15 PRINT "I'M A COMPUTER"
   20 PRINT "SO LONG"
   30 END
   ```

   RUN the program.

9. Before going on to the next exercise, you must erase this program from RAM. To erase a program from the computer's memory, type the command NEW.
   Now type RUN. Does anything happen?
   Type LIST. Is there a program in RAM? No. When you typed NEW, you erased your program from the computer's memory and made room for a *new* program.

Type this. Any line number between 10 and 20 will do.

The apostrophe is above the 7 on the keyboard.

Type RUN.

Type this.

Type this.

Using PRINT Statements

Don't forget
the quotes!

1. Write a program to print your name on the first line of output, your street address on the second line, and your phone number on the third line. Here is part of a sample program.

```
10 PRINT "ROSE VEGA"          ← Type your own name.
20 PRINT ".................."  ← Your street address goes here.
30 PRINT ".................."  ← Your phone number goes here.
```

RUN the program.

Choose a line number ⇨
between 20 and 30.

To take out a line, type ⇨
the line number.

Remember, to change a ⇨
line, just retype the line.

2. Add a line to your program that will print your city and state on the line below your street address. RUN and LIST your program.

3. Take out the line that prints your phone number. Then LIST and RUN your program.

4. Change the line that prints your name so that it prints the name of your brother, sister, pet, or friend. LIST and RUN the program.

5. Type NEW to erase your old program. Then type and RUN this program.

```
10 PRINT "20 + 9 =";
20 PRINT 20 + 9
30 END
```

6. Take out line 20 and change line 10 so that it includes both instructions.

The division sign on the ⇨
keyboard is the slash (/).

7. Type NEW to erase your old program from RAM. Write a program to calculate 543 ÷ 3. (Let the computer do the calculating, not you.)

The multiplication
symbol is the star (*). ⇨

Type NEW before you ⇨
start a new program.

8. Type NEW and write a program to calculate 64 × 4.

9. Type and RUN this program.

```
10 PRINT "ELEGANT";
20 PRINT "ELEPHANTS"
30 PRINT "HUGE",
40 PRINT "HIPPOS"
50 END
```

Be sure your
punctuation marks
are *outside* the
quotation marks.

Type NEW. ⇨

10. Now write and RUN a program with four PRINT statements to give this output.

```
GREENGIRAFFES
YELLOW    YAK
```

Type NEW. ⇨

11. Write and RUN a program which prints COMPUTERS ARE FUN in three zones on the first line of output, and COMPUTERS ARE EASY in three zones on the second line of output. The output will look like this.

```
COMPUTERS    ARE    FUN
COMPUTERS    ARE    EASY
```

Type NEW. ⇨

12. Use PRINT statements to create your own design. Refer to the program you wrote on page 83.

Chapter 15 | JUMPING AROUND

At Your Desk

You know that the computer follows the instructions in a program by starting with the lowest line number, then moving to the next higher number, then the next, and so on. But there is a statement in BASIC that tells the computer to go out of its regular order. Let's see what it is and how it works.

Look at this program. There is a new kind of statement in line 20.

GOTO is a statement in BASIC.

```
1Ø PRINT "HELLO"
2Ø GOTO 4Ø
3Ø PRINT "HAVE A NICE DAY"
4Ø PRINT "GOODBYE"
5Ø END
```

The new statement in line 20, GOTO, means "go to." GOTO 40 means go to line 40. When the computer comes to line 20 and "reads" GOTO 40, it jumps to line 40. It skips right over line 30. What happens to line 30? The computer never "sees" it. HAVE A NICE DAY *does not* get printed. The program and the output look like this.

The computer goes from line 20 to line 40.

```
1Ø PRINT "HELLO"
2Ø GOTO 4Ø
3Ø PRINT "HAVE A NICE DAY"
4Ø PRINT "GOODBYE"
5Ø END
RUN
HELLO
GOODBYE
```

GOTO can make the computer jump all around in a program. The computer can jump "up" as well as "down." Can you tell what the output of this program will be?

Pretend you are the computer. Follow the instructions.

```
10 PRINT "I CAN"
20 GOTO 50
30 PRINT "AROUND!"
40 GOTO 70
50 PRINT "JUMP"
60 GOTO 30
70 END
```

Did you get this output?

```
I CAN
JUMP
AROUND!
```

The program makes the computer read the lines in this order: 10, 20, 50, 60, 30, 40, 70. Let's trace the program.

Line 10 tells the computer to print I CAN.
Line 20 sends the computer to line 50.
Line 50 tells the computer to print JUMP.
Line 60 sends the computer to line 30.
Line 30 tells the computer to print AROUND!
Line 40 sends the computer to line 70.
Line 70 ends the program.

If you are not careful when you use a GOTO statement, you could end up with a program like this.

Can you tell what the output is?

```
10 PRINT "SOMETIMES WE"
20 PRINT "NEVER REACH"
30 GOTO 20
40 PRINT "THE END"
50 END
```

If you follow the instructions carefully, you'll see that the computer cannot get to the end of the program. If you try to write the output, you'll go on forever (so will the computer)!

```
SOMETIMES WE
NEVER REACH
NEVER REACH
NEVER REACH
NEVER REACH
NEVER REACH
NEVER REACH
NEVER REACH
NEVER REACH
```

When the computer gets to line 30, it is sent back to line 20. Then it goes to line 30, and is sent to line 20, and so on. This is called an **infinite loop.**

```
20 PRINT "NEVER REACH"
30 GOTO 20
```

THIS IS MAKING ME DIZZY!

When you plan and write a program, you want the computer to reach the end. Infinite loops in programs are usually programming mistakes, or bugs.

try these

1. Write the output for this program.

```
10 PRINT "MONDAY"
20 PRINT "******"
30 GOTO 50
40 PRINT "TUESDAY"
50 END
```

2. Write the output for this program. It is a rhyme.

```
10 PRINT "I EAT MY PEAS WITH HONEY"
20 GOTO 70
30 PRINT "BUT IT KEEPS THEM ON MY KNIFE"
40 GOTO 90
50 PRINT "IT MAKES THE PEAS TASTE FUNNY"
60 GOTO 30
70 PRINT "I'VE DONE IT ALL MY LIFE"
80 GOTO 50
90 END
```

3. Tell what the bug is in this program by explaining what happens to the output.

```
10 PRINT "LOOK FOR"
20 GOTO 10
30 PRINT "THE BUG"
40 END
```

 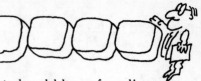

At the Computer

If you make a mistake you can erase it before you press ENTER (or RETURN). Otherwise, retype the line.

Remember, to add a line to a program, type the line.

To list a program, type LIST.

1. Type and RUN this program. Your output should have four lines.

```
10 PRINT "ZANY ZEBRAS"
20 PRINT "WONDERFUL WALRUSES"
30 PRINT "BATTY BATS"
40 PRINT "TICKLISH TURTLES"
50 END
```

2. Now add line 15.

```
15 GOTO 40
```

LIST the program. You should see line 15 between lines 10 and 20.

Now RUN the program. You should have only two lines of output because the computer skips over lines 20 and 30 and does not print WONDERFUL WALRUSES or BATTY BATS. Does your program and output look like this?

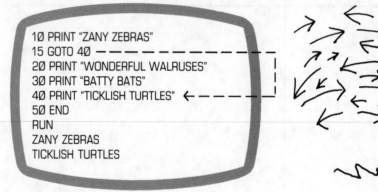

```
10 PRINT "ZANY ZEBRAS"
15 GOTO 40 — — — — — — —
20 PRINT "WONDERFUL WALRUSES"
30 PRINT "BATTY BATS"
40 PRINT "TICKLISH TURTLES" ← — — —
50 END
RUN
ZANY ZEBRAS
TICKLISH TURTLES
```

Remember, to change a line, retype the line.

3. Change line 15 to

```
15 GOTO 50
```

Before you run the program, figure out what will happen. When you think you know what the output will look like, run the program. Did you get this for your output?

```
ZANY ZEBRAS
```

Type NEW to erase your old program before you do this exercise.

4. Type this program. Before you run it, figure out what the output will be. Then run the program.

```
10 PRINT "HELLO"
20 GOTO 50
30 PRINT "GOODBYE"
40 GOTO 70
50 PRINT "HI"
60 GOTO 30
70 PRINT "SO LONG"
80 END
```

Your output should show four lines.

```
HELLO
HI
GOODBYE
SO LONG
```

5. Change line 20 so the output shows:

```
HELLO
SO LONG
```

Find the line that prints SO LONG. Change line 20 so it sends the computer to that line.

6. The next program has an infinite loop. It will make the computer print the output forever. Before you type and run the program, you should know how to stop the computer.

If you have an Apple computer, hold down the CTRL key and press C.

If you have an Atari computer, press BREAK.

If you have a PET computer, press STOP.

If you have a TRS-80 computer, press BREAK.

Now type and RUN this program.

```
10 PRINT "RUNNING"
20 GOTO 10
30 END
```

You should see a column of output. Every time the computer gets to line 20, the GOTO statement sends it back to line 10. Now *stop* the computer. Then type LIST to list your program on the screen.

7. Add this line to your program and run it.

```
15 PRINT "FOREVER"
```

You may not be able to read the output because the computer is printing it so fast—but it is printing this over and over:

```
RUNNING
FOREVER
RUNNING
FOREVER
RUNNING
FOREVER
RUNNING
FOREVER
```

Stop the computer and type NEW to erase your program.

8. You can have fun with infinite loops and punctuation marks. Do you remember what a semicolon does in a PRINT statement?

Here is a hint.

Remember, **infinite** means "never ending."

If you don't have one of these machines, ask your teacher to show you how to stop the computer.

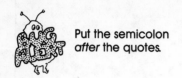
Put the semicolon *after* the quotes.

Type and RUN this program.

```
1Ø PRINT "ALICE";   ←————————————— Type your name in the
2Ø GOTO 1Ø                          quotes.
3Ø END
```

WOW! Are you getting your name all over the screen? Stop the program and LIST it. The semicolon certainly makes a big difference. Remember, a semicolon tells the computer to *continue the output on the same line.* Each time the computer printed your name, it printed it right next to the "old" name on the same line. When the output reaches the end of a line, it continues on the next line:

```
ALICEALICEALICEALICEALICEALICE
ALICEALICEALICEALICEALICEALICE
ALICEALICEALICEALICEALICEALICE
ALICEALICEALICEALICEALICEALICE
ALICEALICEALICEALICEALICEALICE
ALICEALICEALICEALICEALICEALICE
ALICEALICEALICEALICEALICEALICE
ALICEALICEALICEALICEALICEALICE
```

9. You can make your name a little easier to read. Change line 10 to:

```
1Ø PRINT "ALICE ";                   Leave a space here.
```

Remember, the computer will print whatever is inside the quotes, including the space. Now RUN the program. Do you see a space between each name? That's because you instructed the computer to print the space, by putting it in the quotes. Stop the computer and LIST your program.

10. Let's see what a comma does. Change line 10 to:

```
1Ø PRINT "ALICE",
```

RUN the program, then stop it. Remember, a comma tells the computer to *continue its output in the next zone.* The first time through the loop, the computer printed ALICE in the first zone, the second time in the second zone, the third time in the third zone, and so on. When there were no more zones the computer continued printing on the next line. Your name was printed in columns on the screen.

Remember, type *your* name.

Remember that different computers have different numbers of zones.

Some computers indent each new line when printing in zones. You may not have "straight" columns.

11. Type NEW. Write a program to print BOO in a column down the screen. (Use exercise 6 as a guide.)

12. Type NEW. Write a program that will make the computer continue to print a word in zones. Choose the word you want printed. Use one PRINT statement with a comma.

13. Type NEW. Write a program to print rows of stars all over the screen. You need only one star in your program.

What punctuation mark should you use?

Chapter 16 | ADDRESSES

At Your Desk

In this chapter, you will see how the computer's Random Access Memory stores specific pieces of information. RAM contains thousands of storage units, called address locations. They are represented by electrical circuits on an integrated circuit chip. You cannot see these address locations since they are electrical circuits. It helps if you imagine them as little mailboxes.

The mailboxes on your street might have names on them such as:

Computer address locations can also be given names. Each name is usually one letter of the alphabet.

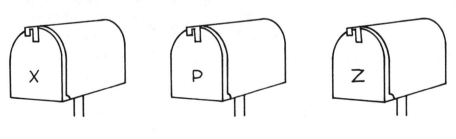

Using LET Statements

LET is a statement in BASIC.

Look at this statement:

    10 LET X = 4

It means that you are going to call one of the computer's address locations X and store a 4 in it. What do you think these statements mean?

    20 LET P = 12
    30 LET Z = 24

Line 20 means that another address location will be called P, and a 12 will be stored in it. Line 30 means that 24 will be stored in an address location named Z. To remember how these LET statements work, try to imagine that the computer's address locations are "mailboxes." Three of them are named X, P, and Z. They are storing the numbers 4, 12, and 24.

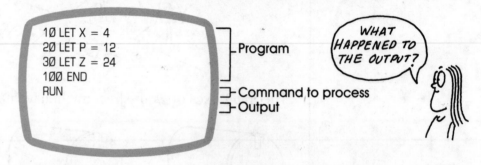

Let's put these three lines into a computer program. Here's what the program and its output would look like on a computer screen.

The *name* of the address location is on the *left* side of the equal sign. The *number stored* is on the right.

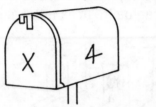 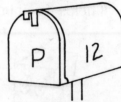 

Program
Command to process
Output

Remember, all of this data is stored in RAM.

There's nothing in the output! Why? Didn't the computer do anything? The computer did just what we told it to do. It *stored* a 4 in the X address location. It *stored* a 12 in the P address location. It *stored* a 24 in the Z address location. But it did not *display* anything. The statement LET means "store." It does not display anything on the screen. You need a PRINT statement in the program if you want something displayed. If you want to see what is stored in the address locations, you need to add line 40 to the program. Now see what you get when you RUN the program.

```
10 LET X = 4
20 LET P = 12
30 LET Z = 24
40 PRINT X, P, Z
100 END
RUN
4          12          24
```

YOU COULD HAVE USED:
40 PRINT X,
41 PRINT P,
42 PRINT Z,
BUT 40 PRINT X, P, Z IS
EASIER TO TYPE.

Line 40 instructs the computer to print the *number* stored in X, the *number* stored in P, and the *number* stored in Z.

How did the computer know to print the numbers stored in the X, P, and Z address locations, and not the letters X, P, and Z? Let's add line 50 to this program and see if you can find the answer.

```
10 LET X = 4
20 LET P = 12
30 LET Z = 24
40 PRINT X, P, Z
50 PRINT "X", "P", "Z"
100 END
RUN
4          12          24
X          P          Z
```

You can see that line 50 has *quotation marks* around the letters, and line 40 does not. So, the output for line 50 is the three letters in the quotes—X, P, Z. In line 40, the letters are *not* in quotes. So the computer prints the numbers stored in these address locations—4, 12, and 24.

So far, address locations have been named with one letter of the alphabet. Most computers allow you to use more than one letter.

The name of an address location must not contain a word in the BASIC language. You can't use the word LETTER because it contains the word LET.

Here is an example. ⇨

```
10 LET XYZ = 9
```

You can also use letters and numbers to name an address location.

An address location must begin with a letter. You cannot use 2B as an address location.

Here is an example. ⇨

```
10 LET K32L = 15
```

99

If you look at a program that someone has written, you may see address location names with more than one letter. In this book you will see single letters used. This is so you can avoid bugs when you write programs.

1. Write the output for each program.

   a. 10 LET A = 12
   20 PRINT A
   30 END

   b. 10 LET A = 12
   20 PRINT A
   30 PRINT "A"
   40 END

2. In program 1b, explain the difference between lines 20 and 30.

3. What is the bug in this program? Tell how to fix it.

   ```
   10 LET 25 = S
   20 LET T = 33
   30 PRINT S, T
   40 END
   ```

4. **a.** Write the output for the program below.
   b. Why is the number 4 not in the output?

   ```
   10 LET G = 2
   20 LET H = 4
   30 PRINT "THE NUMBER STORED IN G IS "
   40 PRINT G
   50 END
   ```

5. Write a program to store 5 in address location D and 8 in location E. The output should look like:

   ```
   D          E
   5          8
   ```

Using Stored Numbers

Let's see how you can use numbers stored in address locations. This program shows you how to calculate with stored numbers.

Look at lines 30 and 40.

```
10 LET A = 14
20 LET B = 7
30 PRINT A + B, A − B
40 PRINT A * B, A/B
50 END
RUN
21          7
98          2
```

Line 30 tells the computer to calculate and print the value of A + B in zone 1 and the value of A − B in zone 2. To calculate A + B, the computer "looks" in address location A and "sees" a 14. Then it "looks" in B and "sees" a 7. Then it adds 14 and 7, and prints the answer 21. The computer then does the same thing to calculate A − B. In line 40, the computer calculates A * B and A/B in the same way and prints the answers.

Since there are no quotes around A + B, the computer calculates and prints the answer.

You can change what is stored in an address location. Look at this program and the output:

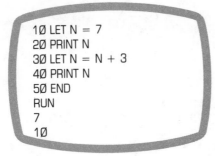

```
10 LET N = 7
20 PRINT N
30 LET N = N + 3
40 PRINT N
50 END
RUN
7
10
```

You know that line 10 tells the computer to store a 7 in the address location N. Line 20 tells the computer to print whatever is stored in N. What do you think line 30 means?

30 LET N = N + 3

Line 30 tells the computer to store a new number in N. The computer starts with the number already in N—the 7—and adds 3 to it. Then it stores the new number, 10, in N. In other words, the 7 is being replaced by the 10. Line 40 tells the computer to print whatever is in N—the 10.

You can change the number stored in an address location as many times as you need to. Here is a program that changes the stored number over and over again.

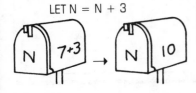

```
10 LET S = 1
20 PRINT S
30 LET S = S + 1
40 GOTO 20
```

THERE'S NO END STATEMENT TO THIS PROGRAM.

IT WOULDN'T DO ANY GOOD. THIS PROGRAM MAKES AN INFINITE LOOP.

Line 10 stores 1 in the S address location.

Line 20 prints what is stored in S, which is 1.

Line 30 adds 1 more to the number in S. 1 + 1 = 2, so now 2 is stored in S.

Line 40 sends the computer back to line 20.

Line 20 prints what is stored in S, which is 2—and so on.

As you can see, the computer keeps adding 1 more to the S address location. Then it prints the new number. There is an *infinite loop* in the program that keeps the computer "counting" forever. *But,*

Let's trace the program.

The output will be a column of numbers that "roll" off the screen and come up from the bottom of the screen:
1
2
3
.
.
.

The infinite loop is from line 40 to line 20.

computers *do* have a limit. They will only work with numbers up to a certain size. Then they stop. Some microcomputers will work with numbers that are up to 38 digits long!

Lines 30, 50, and 70 change the number stored in S.

There are four PRINT statements. You should have four lines of output.

There is no punctuation mark in line 20. The output will be a column of numbers.

1. Write the output for this program.

```
10 LET X = 12
20 LET Y = 4
30 PRINT X + Y, X − Y
40 PRINT X * Y, X/Y
50 END
```

2. Write the output.

```
10 LET S = 24
20 PRINT S
30 LET S = S/6
40 PRINT S
50 LET S = S * 4
60 PRINT S
70 LET S = S − 10
80 PRINT S
90 END
```

3. Write the output until you find the pattern. What kind of numbers does the output show?

```
10 LET A = 0
20 PRINT A
30 LET A = A + 2
40 GOTO 20
```

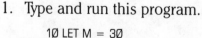

At the Computer

1. Type and run this program.

```
10 LET M = 30
20 LET N = 5
30 PRINT "M", "N"
40 PRINT M, N
100 END
```

Your output should look like this.

```
M          N
3Ø         5
```

2. Add these two lines to your program. Then type LIST to put the lines in order.

```
5Ø PRINT M + N
6Ø PRINT M * N
```

Now run the program. You should get this output.

```
M          N
3Ø         5
35
15Ø
```

30 + 5 = 35 ⟹
30 * 5 = 150

3. Change lines 10 and 20 to:

```
1Ø LET M = 1ØØ
2Ø LET N = 5Ø
```

Can you tell what the new output will be? Run the program.

4. Most computers allow you to leave out the word LET in a statement.

A = 5 is the same as LET A = 5.

Type and run this program.

```
1Ø A = 375
2Ø B = 961
3Ø C = A + B
4Ø PRINT "THE SUM OF "; A; " AND "; B; " IS "; C
5Ø END
```

Type NEW to erase your ⟹ old program.

Leave spaces as ⟹ shown here so you have spaces between the words in the output.

Does your output look like this? If not, go back and fix your program.

THE SUM OF 375 AND 961 IS 1336

5. Change lines 10 and 20 in the program above to:

```
1Ø A = 1ØØ
2Ø B = 1ØØ
```

Then run the program. Did you get the output you expected?

6. Choose your own numbers to store in A and B. Change lines 10 and 20 again, so your own numbers are stored in A and B. Run the program.

Remember to erase ⟹ your old program first.

7. Type and run this program. It changes the number stored in Z.

```
1Ø LET Z = 8
2Ø PRINT Z,
3Ø LET Z = Z + 3
4Ø PRINT Z,
¹ØØ END
```

The comma in line 20 makes the computer print the output from line 40 in the next *zone*.

If you forget how to stop the computer, look at page 95.

Retype line 20.

Hint—Let X equal the first number you want to print: LET X = 0

Hint—What do you have to do to get from 100 to 99? From 99 to 98? Subtract 1 each time.

Hint—How do you get from 2 to 4? From 4 to 8? From 8 to 16? Multiply by 2!

Scientific notation is also used to write very small numbers—numbers less than 1 that are very close to 0.

E stands for "exponent." This number really means 3.425×10^6. (10^6 is 1,000,000.)

Did you get 8 in the first zone and 11 in the second zone?

8. Add these lines to your program and run the program.

```
5Ø LET Z = Z − 5
6Ø PRINT Z
```

Line 50 instructs the computer to subtract 5 from Z. The last number in Z was 11, so Z now is 11 − 5, or 6. Line 60 tells the computer to print whatever is in Z, which is now 6.

9. Type NEW. Type and run this program.

```
1Ø LET X = 1
2Ø PRINT X
3Ø LET X = X + 1
4Ø GOTO 2Ø
```

What is happening? Every time the computer goes through the GOTO loop, it adds one more to the number in the address location. First X stores a 1, and then the computer prints it. Then the computer adds one more. So X stores a 2, and the computer prints it—and so on.

10. What punctuation mark could you add to your program so your output goes across the screen, instead of down? Add a semicolon to the end of the PRINT statement—line 20. Run the program again.

11. Write a program to print the even numbers starting with 0. The beginning of your output should be: 0, 2, 4, 6, 8, . . .

12. Now write a program to print the numbers starting with 100 going down one at a time: 100, 99, 98, 97, 96, etc. Watch what happens to the numbers after they get below 0!

13. Write a program to print numbers that have this pattern: 2, 4, 8, 16, 32, 64, 128. The numbers should be in a column. Let this program run for a while, and you will see something strange happen to the numbers in the output. Most computers write large numbers, usually over 1,000,000, in a special shorthand called **scientific notation.** Here is an example of a number written in scientific notation:

```
3.425E + Ø6
```

Here is an easy way to tell what number this is. Look at the number after the E. + 06 means you should move the decimal point six places to the right.

```
3.425E + Ø6 = 342500Ø.
```

You will not come across scientific notation very often in your output, but when you do, remember it is only a shorthand way of writing very large or very small numbers.

Chapter 17 STRINGING ALONG

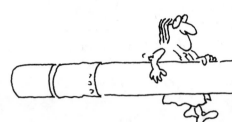

At Your Desk

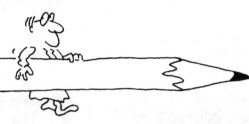

You have learned how a computer can store numbers in address locations. A computer can also store words. A word or any group of characters that is not a number, is called a **string.** These are strings:

```
TODAY         RAINBOW
COMPUTER      FORMULA 280Z
```

When you want to store a string, you must let the computer know a string is coming (instead of a number). You add a dollar sign ($) to the end of the address location's name. Also, you must put quotes around the string.

Read this as: "Let A-string equal blue."

```
LET A$ = "BLUE"

LET P$ = "GOOD MORNING!"

LET C$ = "!!!***###"
```

If you try to store a string without quotes, you'll have a bug in your program.

Most computers allow you to use more than one letter or number (followed by $) to name a string address location:

```
LET D5E6$ = "CATS AND DOGS"
```

You can't start a string address location with a number, and you can't use a word in the BASIC language.

But the rules that hold for number address locations also hold for strings. In this book, you will see a single letter with a dollar sign used. This is so you can avoid bugs when you name strings.

Number address locations and string address locations are entirely different locations in the computer's memory. Look at this program.

Remember, the name of the address location goes on the left side of the equal sign.

```
10 LET A = 25
20 LET A$ = "DOODLES"
30 PRINT A, A$
40 END
RUN
25        DOODLES
```

Let's trace the program.

Line 10 stores the number 25 in address location A. (It doesn't print anything.)

105

Line 20 stores the string DOODLES in address location A$. (It doesn't print anything.)

Line 30 prints the contents of A in the first zone, and the contents of A$ in the second zone.

As you can see, A and A$ are not the same.

This section is for Atari computer users.

If you use an Atari microcomputer, here are some special instructions for you. If you are going to use strings in a program, you must reserve space for the strings. To reserve space, start your program with a statement like this:

```
5 DIM A$(20)
```

DIM stands for "dimension." DIM is a statement in BASIC.

This statement reserves enough room in the computer's memory for you to put as many as 20 characters in the string called A$. (You can use less than 20, but not more.) You can always reserve "extra" space. If you think A$ might hold a string longer than 20 characters, you can type:

```
5 DIM A$(50)
```

Don't use too large a number in parentheses. You might use up too much RAM space. Then you won't have enough room for the rest of your program.

This statement lets you store as many as 50 characters in A$.

If you are going to use more than one string in your program, you can reserve room for them in just one DIM statement:

```
5 DIM A$(20), B$(15), C$(30)
```

This section is for everyone.

Line 5 is for the Atari computer.

Remember, you do not have to use the word LET.

You can use PRINT statements to print strings in any order. Look at this program.

```
5 DIM W$(15), J$(10), P$(10)
10 P = 3
20 W$ = " WATERMELONS"
30 J$ = " JUICY"
40 P$ = " PINK"
50 PRINT P; P$; J$; W$
60 END
```

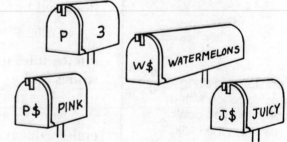

If you ran this program, the output would look like this:

```
3 PINK JUICY WATERMELONS
```

Look at line 50. First, it prints the number stored in P. Then, it prints the string stored in address location P$. Next, the computer prints what is stored in J$. Then, it prints what is stored in W$ on the same line.

WHY ARE THERE SPACES BETWEEN THE WORDS? I THOUGHT THE SEMICOLONS TOLD THE COMPUTER TO CONTINUE THE OUTPUT IN THE NEXT SPACE.

LOOK AT THE STRINGS IN LINES 20, 30, AND 40. THERE IS A SPACE BEFORE EACH WORD, AND THE SPACE IS _INSIDE_ THE QUOTES. SO THE COMPUTER PRINTS THE SPACE ALONG WITH THE WORD.

You can use a plus sign (+) to tell the computer to put strings together.

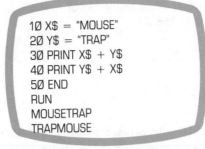

```
10 X$ = "MOUSE"
20 Y$ = "TRAP"
30 PRINT X$ + Y$
40 PRINT Y$ + X$
50 END
RUN
MOUSETRAP
TRAPMOUSE
```

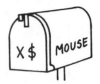 

The Atari computer does not put strings together in this way. If you have one, use a semicolon (;) instead of the plus sign (+) in lines 30 and 40.

Line 30 tells the computer to put the strings stored in X$ and Y$ together and print them. Line 40 means put the strings in Y$ and X$ together and print them in that order. Putting strings together with a plus sign (+) is called **concatenating.**

You can store concatenated strings in address locations. Look at this program.

Concatenate (kon kat' ə nāt) means "link together."

If you have an Atari computer, omit line 30 and change line 40 to: PRINT X$; Y$

```
10 X$ = "MOUSE"
20 Y$ = "TRAP"
30 Z$ = X$ + Y$
40 PRINT Z$
50 END
```

Line 30 tells the computer to store X$ + Y$, or MOUSETRAP, in address location Z$. Line 40 has the computer print what is stored in Z$. So, the output is:

```
MOUSETRAP
```

1. Each statement has a bug in it. Find the bug. Then write the statement correctly.

   a. LET C$ = CARROTS
   b. "COMPUTER" = A$
   c. Z = "ZEBRA"

2. Write the output.

```
5 DIM A$(15)
10 LET A = 100
20 LET A$ = " FRENCH FRIES"
30 PRINT A; A$
40 END
```

Line 5 is for Atari computer users only.

Continued

3. Use a PRINT statement in line 50 with correct punctuation marks so you get this output: MYWORDSRUNTOGETHER

Line 5 is for Atari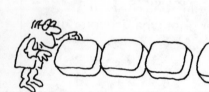
computer users only.

```
5 DIM W$(7), R$(5), M$(5), T$(1Ø)
1Ø W$ = "WORDS"
2Ø R$ = "RUN"
3Ø M$ = "MY"
4Ø T$ = "TOGETHER"
5Ø
6Ø END
```

4. If you do *not* use an Atari computer, write the output for a. If you use an Atari computer, write the output for b.

Notice the spaces in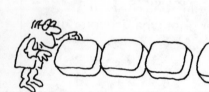
lines 20 and 30. The
words won't run together
in the output.

a.
```
1Ø X$ = "STRINGS ARE"
2Ø Y$ = " EASY"
3Ø Z$ = " FUN"
4Ø PRINT X$ + Y$
5Ø PRINT X$ + Z$
6Ø END
```

b.
```
5 DIM X$(15), Y$(5), Z$(5)
1Ø X$ = "STRINGS ARE"
2Ø Y$ = " EASY"
3Ø Z$ = " FUN"
4Ø PRINT X$; Y$
5Ø PRINT X$; Z$
6Ø END
```

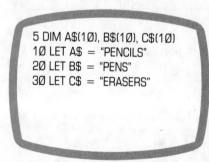

At the Computer

You have learned how the computer stores strings in string address locations. Now let's put some strings into your computer!

1. Type and run this program:

Line 5 is for Atari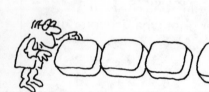
computer users only.

```
5 DIM A$(1Ø), B$(1Ø), C$(1Ø)
1Ø LET A$ = "PENCILS"
2Ø LET B$ = "PENS"
3Ø LET C$ = "ERASERS"
```

THERE'S NOTHING IN THE OUTPUT!

What did you get for the output? You only *stored* strings in address locations. You didn't tell the computer to print anything. Now add these lines to your program. Run it again.

```
4Ø PRINT A$, B$, C$
5Ø PRINT C$, A$, B$
6Ø PRINT B$, C$, A$
```

Your output should look like this:

```
PENCILS    PENS      ERASERS ←——————— Output from line 40
ERASERS    PENCILS   PENS    ←——————— Output from line 50
PENS       ERASERS   PENCILS ←——————— Output from line 60
```

Did you notice there is no END statement in this program? When the computer has no more instructions to follow, it automatically ENDs.

2. Before you type and run this program, type NEW to erase your old program.

Line 5 is for Atari computer users only.

Be sure to include spaces where you see them.

```
5 DIM Q$(10), R$(10)
10 Q$ = " PEPERONI"
20 R$ = " PIZZAS"
30 S = 13
40 PRINT S; Q$; R$
```

WHERE ARE THE QUOTES AND DOLLAR SIGN IN LINE 30?

A NUMBER IS BEING STORED— NOT A STRING.

Did you get this output?

```
13 PEPERONI PIZZAS
```

3. Symbols can be used in strings, too. Type and run this program.

Erase your old program first.

Line 5 is for Atari computer users.

```
5 DIM L$(50), S$(20)
10 LET L$ = "**********LONG STRING**********"
20 LET S$ = "*SHORT STRING*"
30 PRINT S$
40 PRINT L$
```

You will not see DIM statements at the beginning of programs in the rest of this book. Remember, every time you use strings in a program, you must *dimension* them (reserve space). Use a DIM statement in the first line of your program.

Note for Atari computer users.

4. You can change what's stored in a string address location by putting a new string in the same address location. Type and run this program:

Type NEW.

```
10 S = 5
20 S$ = " SMALL TADPOLES"
30 PRINT S; S$
40 S$ = " BIG FROGS"
50 PRINT S; S$
```

Remember to check for typing mistakes before you enter each line.

In Line 30, when the computer prints S and S$, S is 5 and S$ is SMALL TADPOLES. In line 50, when the computer prints S and S$, S is still 5 and S$ is now BIG FROGS.

5. Remember that strings can be **concatenated**, or "added" together. Type this program. Try to figure out the output before you run the program.

Type NEW.

```
10 A$ = " BERRIES"
20 B$ = " NUTS"
30 C$ = " AND"
40 X$ = A$ + C$ + B$
50 Y$ = B$ + C$ + A$
60 PRINT X$
70 PRINT Y$
```

Atari computer users: omit lines 40 and 50. Change lines 60 and 70 to:
60 PRINT A$; C$; B$
70 PRINT B$; C$; A$

Type NEW.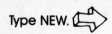

Atari computer users: just add a PRINT statement.

Type NEW.

What punctuation mark will display the output in zones?

Atari computer users need to use a DIM statement.

6. Write a program to store your first name in one address location, and your last name in another address location. Using the address locations, instruct the computer to print an output like this:

MIKE   KRAMER
KRAMER   MIKE

Use the correct punctuation mark to print the names in zones.

7. Add a line to the program above to **concatenate** your first and last names, so that one address location is storing both names. Then add another line to print what is in the new address location.

8. Write a program to store each of these words in address locations:

DIAMOND   APPLE   CRAYON

Then have the computer print these words in alphabetical order in three zones.

9. In this program, you'll use all the statements you have learned so far. Type NEW. Type and run:

```
10 LET X = 1
20 LET X$ = " STRINGS ARE FUN"
30 PRINT X; X$
40 LET X = X + 1
50 GOTO 30
```

While it's running, trace the program and figure out what's happening. Line 50 keeps sending the computer back to line 30. Each time through this loop, the computer adds 1 more to X. It prints the number stored in X and the string stored in X$.

Stop the program.

THOSE NUMBERS ARE GETTING VERY LARGE! I HOPE YOU REMEMBER HOW TO STOP A PROGRAM. IF NOT, LOOK AT PAGE 95.

Chapter 18 | TALKING BACK

At Your Desk

Have you ever used a computer to play a game, practice math facts, or take a quiz? If so, you have seen the computer ask a question, then wait for your answer. In this chapter, you will learn how the computer accepts your answers, even though they are not part of the program itself.

Look at this program. There is a new statement in line 20.

INPUT is a statement in the BASIC language.

```
10 PRINT "WHAT'S YOUR NAME?"
20 INPUT N$
40 END
RUN
WHAT'S YOUR NAME?
?
```

You know that line 10 prints WHAT'S YOUR NAME? on the screen. Line 20 has a new statement called INPUT. INPUT tells the computer to *stop, print a question mark on the screen*, and *wait* for the **user** to type in a response. The user's response gets stored in the address location N$. Let's suppose Harry walks up to the computer and sees the output on the screen above. So, he types in his name—HARRY. The computer screen would look like this.

The user is the person using the program. The user can be the person who wrote the program or someone else.

```
10 PRINT "WHAT'S YOUR NAME?"
20 INPUT N$
40 END
RUN
WHAT'S YOUR NAME?
?HARRY
```

The computer printed the question mark. → ?HARRY ← Harry typed his name.

After Harry hits the ENTER (or RETURN) key, the computer moves to the next line, which ENDs the program. Let's make the program more interesting by adding another line, line 30. When Harry runs the program it looks like this.

```
10 PRINT "WHAT'S YOUR NAME?"
20 INPUT N$
30 PRINT "HELLO, "; N$
40 END
RUN
WHAT'S YOUR NAME?
?HARRY
HELLO, HARRY
```

After Harry types his name and enters it, the computer stores his name and moves to line 30. Line 30 tells the computer to print HELLO, a comma, and a space. The semicolon continues the output on the same line. Then the computer prints what is stored in N$— HARRY. So, the output from line 30 is HELLO, HARRY.

Suppose Robin runs the same program. When she sees WHAT'S YOUR NAME? on the screen, she types in ROBIN. ROBIN gets stored in address location N$. The output looks like this:

```
WHAT'S YOUR NAME?
?ROBIN
HELLO, ROBIN
```

Harry, Robin, and anyone else who runs this program are the users. The INPUT statement allows a user to store information in an address location. When you type this program, nothing is stored in N$. The computer doesn't put anything in N$ until the program is run. Every time the program is run, the user can store something new in N$.

Here's another program that uses INPUT statements. Look at the program and the output.

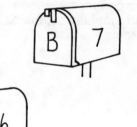

```
10 PRINT "TYPE A NUMBER"
20 INPUT A
30 PRINT "TYPE ANOTHER NUMBER"
40 INPUT B
50 PRINT "THE SUM OF YOUR NUMBERS IS "; A + B
RUN
TYPE A NUMBER
?6
TYPE ANOTHER NUMBER
?7
THE SUM OF YOUR NUMBERS IS 13
```

Another output might be:

```
TYPE A NUMBER
?123
TYPE ANOTHER NUMBER
?234
THE SUM OF YOUR NUMBERS IS 357
```

Let's trace the program:

Line 10 tells the computer to print TYPE A NUMBER on the screen.

Line 20 tells the computer to stop and wait for the user to type a response. The user's response will be stored in A.

Line 30 tells the computer to print TYPE ANOTHER NUMBER on the screen.

Line 40 tells the computer to stop and wait for the user to type another response. That response will be stored in B.

Line 50 tells the computer to print THE SUM OF YOUR NUMBERS IS. The semicolon means continue the output on the same line. The computer prints the answer to A + B.

You can write a program for a Computer Ad Lib game using INPUT and PRINT statements. Here's an example of how the game works. In Computer Ad Lib, you are asked several questions. Then, your answers are used in a short story. Here are some questions.

What's your name?
Name an action verb.
Where would you like to visit?
Name an animal.

Pretend your name is Jennifer. You chose "jump" as your action verb. You named "Alaska" as a place you would like to visit. You named "camel" as an animal. Your Computer Ad Lib would read:

Jennifer decided to jump all the way to Alaska on a camel!

Here is a program for the Computer Ad Lib.

```
10 PRINT "WHAT'S YOUR NAME?"
20 INPUT N$
30 PRINT "NAME AN ACTION VERB."
40 INPUT V$
50 PRINT "WHERE WOULD YOU LIKE TO VISIT?"
60 INPUT W$
70 PRINT "NAME AN ANIMAL."
80 INPUT A$
90 PRINT
100 PRINT N$; " DECIDED TO "; V$; " ALL THE WAY TO "; W$; " ON A "; A$;"!"
```

THE PRINT STATEMENTS ASK THE QUESTIONS.

THE INPUT STATEMENTS ALLOW THE USER TO PUT IN ANSWERS.

Lines 10, 30, 50, and 70 print something on the screen. Lines 20, 40, 60, and 80 instruct the computer to stop and wait for the user's response. Each response is stored in an address location. Line 90 leaves a line of space. Line 100 is a long PRINT statement. Let's examine it carefully.

```
100 PRINT N$; " DECIDED TO "; V$; " ALL THE WAY TO "; W$; " ON A "; A$;"!"
```

Every time a different person answers the questions, the story changes.

Atari computer users need a DIM statement for N$, V$, W$, and A$.

Line 90 "prints" one line of space.

On some computers you can leave out the semicolons.

The computer prints all the words in quotes, exactly as they are written—including the spaces. It also prints the exclamation point at the end of the sentence. Every time the computer sees the name of an address location, it will print whatever is stored in that address location.

If Jennifer were to run this program on the computer, it would store:

JENNIFER in address location N$.
JUMP in address location V$.
ALASKA in address location W$.
CAMEL in address location A$.

Then the computer would print:

JENNIFER DECIDED TO JUMP ALL THE WAY TO ALASKA ON A CAMEL!

If Phil ran this program on a computer and answered PHIL, SWIM, THE NORTH POLE, and HIPPOPOTAMUS, it would print:

PHIL DECIDED TO SWIM ALL THE WAY TO THE NORTH POLE ON A HIPPOPOTAMUS!

1. Find the bugs in this part of a program. Tell how to fix them.

```
10 PRINT "WHAT'S YOUR FAVORITE COLOR?"
20 INPUT C
30 PRINT "NAME YOUR LUCKY NUMBER."
40 INPUT N$
```

2. Write the output for this program. Since you will be the *user*, put your own name in the output.

Be sure to show the question mark and the user's response in your output.

```
10 PRINT "WHAT'S YOUR NAME?"
20 INPUT N$
30 PRINT N$; " SPEAKS BASIC."
```

3. Write the output for this program. Fill in whatever numbers you wish for the user's responses.

To make things easier, pick a larger number for your first response.

```
10 PRINT "NAME A NUMBER."
20 INPUT A
30 PRINT "NAME ANOTHER NUMBER."
40 INPUT B
50 PRINT "THE SUM OF YOUR NUMBERS IS "; A + B
60 PRINT "THE DIFFERENCE BETWEEN YOUR NUMBERS IS "; A - B
```

4. Here is a Computer Ad Lib program. For lines 10-160, answer each question. Write the output for lines 170-250. You'll have a Computer Ad Lib!

To help you remember your answers for the Ad Lib, write each address location and what you stored in it.

```
10 PRINT "WHAT'S YOUR NAME?"
20 INPUT N$
30 PRINT "HOW OLD ARE YOU?"
```

```
40 INPUT A
50 PRINT "NAME A LARGE FOUR-LEGGED ANIMAL."
60 INPUT A$
70 PRINT "NAME A PART OF YOUR BODY."
80 INPUT B$
90 PRINT "NAME AN ADJECTIVE."
100 INPUT J$
110 PRINT "ANOTHER ADJECTIVE, PLEASE."
120 INPUT K$
130 PRINT "AND NOW, NAME A VEGETABLE (PLURAL)."
140 INPUT V$
150 PRINT "FINALLY, GIVE THE LAST NAME OF A FAMOUS PERSON."
160 INPUT F$
170 PRINT "NOW FOR YOUR COMPUTER AD LIB . . ."
180 PRINT
190 PRINT "DEAR DR. "; F$
200 PRINT "       MY PET "; A$; " SEEMS TO BE ILL."
210 PRINT "HE HAS SEVERAL "; V$; " GROWING OUT OF HIS "; B$
220 PRINT "HE'S USUALLY A VERY "; J$; " PET, BUT LATELY HE'S BEEN ACTING "; K$
230 PRINT "PLEASE TELL ME WHAT TO DO BECAUSE I HAVE "; A; " OTHER "; A$;
        "S IN THE HOUSE AND MY MOTHER IS GETTING MAD."
240 PRINT "                         SINCERELY,"
250 PRINT "                         "; N$
```

A PRINT statement with nothing after it "prints" a line of space.

Don't forget to include the spaces inside the quotes in your output.

At the Computer

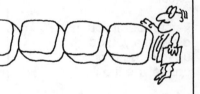

Atari computer users need to type:
5 DIM Y$(30)

Be sure to leave a space after the comma in line 30.

1. Type and RUN this program:

   ```
   10 PRINT "HELLO, I'M YOUR FRIENDLY COMPUTER. WHO ARE YOU?"
   20 INPUT Y$
   30 PRINT "GLAD TO MEET YOU, "; Y$
   ```

   After the computer prints HELLO, I'M YOUR FRIENDLY COMPUTER. WHO ARE YOU?, a question mark appears on the screen and the computer stops and waits for your response. When you enter your response, it is stored in Y$. When the computer prints GLAD TO MEET YOU, it should add your name to the end of the message. RUN the program several times, putting in a different response each time.

2. Add these lines to your program:

   ```
   40 PRINT "HOW OLD ARE YOU, "; Y$
   50 INPUT X
   60 PRINT X; " YEARS OLD - - - WOW!"
   ```

   Run the program. After you type your age, the computer moves to line 60 and substitutes your age for X.

3. Now add:

```
70 PRINT "THAT'S "; X*12; " MONTHS!"
80 PRINT "THAT'S "; X*365; " DAYS!"
90 PRINT "THAT'S "; X*365*24; " HOURS!"
100 PRINT "YOU'RE PRETTY OLD, "; Y$
```

Do not use quotes around the calculations. You want the computer to print the *answers*.

In line 70, your age (stored in X) is multiplied by 12, since there are 12 months in a year. In line 80, your age is multiplied by 365 since there are 365 days in a year. In line 90, your age is multiplied by 365×24. This gives the number of hours you have lived. RUN the program using your correct age. Then RUN it a few more times, putting in other ages.

4. Type this program.

```
10 PRINT "I CAN ADD ANY TWO NUMBERS."
20 PRINT "GIVE ME ONE NUMBER."
30 INPUT X
40 PRINT "GIVE ME ANOTHER NUMBER."
50 INPUT Y
60 PRINT "THE SUM OF "; X; " AND "; Y; " IS "; X + Y
```

Run the program several times, using different numbers each time.

5. Type and run this Computer Ad Lib program.

```
10 PRINT "WHAT'S YOUR NAME?"
20 INPUT N$
30 PRINT "NAME AN OBJECT YOU HAVE AT SCHOOL"
40 INPUT S$
50 PRINT "WHAT DO YOU LIKE FOR LUNCH?"
60 INPUT L$
70 PRINT "MY TEACHER SAID,"
80 PRINT N$; "! GET THAT "; S$; " OUT OF YOUR "; L$
90 END
```

Run the program several times. Each time, ask yourself, "What is the computer storing in N$, S$, and L$?" The computer prints the strings stored in N$, S$, and L$ when it gets to line 80.

6. Write a program that asks the user's age. Then have the computer tell how old the user was last year, and how old the user will be next year. Here is a sample output for a user who is 9 years old:

```
HOW OLD ARE YOU?
?9
LAST YEAR YOU WERE 8
NEXT YEAR YOU WILL BE 10
```

Type NEW.

7. Write a program that asks the user for two numbers and prints the difference between those two numbers. Here is a sample output for a user who chooses 99 and 3:

```
WHAT IS YOUR FIRST NUMBER?
?99
WHAT IS YOUR SECOND NUMBER?
?3
THE DIFFERENCE BETWEEN YOUR NUMBERS IS 96
```

You can use exercise 5 as a guide.

8. Write a Computer Ad Lib. First, think of a short story or sentence that has three or four key words that you can store in address locations. Then, ask three or four questions with PRINT statements. Each PRINT statement should be followed by an INPUT statement to store the answer. After your three or four PRINTs and INPUTs, you will need some PRINT statements to write your "story." Remember to use the address locations in place of the key words.

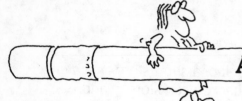

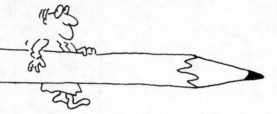

At Your Desk

Look at the output on this computer screen.

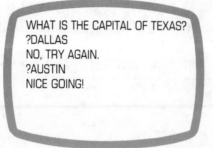

```
WHAT IS THE CAPITAL OF TEXAS?
?DALLAS
NO, TRY AGAIN.
?AUSTIN
NICE GOING!
```

How did the computer decide whether the user's answer was right? You know that the computer cannot make these kinds of decisions by itself. The decisions must be programmed. In this chapter you will learn how to program your computer so it will respond to an answer.

Look at these two lines of a program.

```
10 PRINT "WHICH WOULD YOU LIKE, A DAISY OR A DANDELION?"
20 INPUT C$
```

Remember, the **user** is the person running the program.

You know that the computer will print WHICH WOULD YOU LIKE, A DAISY OR A DANDELION? on the screen. Then, it will stop and wait for the user to type in an answer. That answer will be stored in the C$ address location.

Let's add more lines to the program. There is a new statement in line 30 and line 40.

IF-THEN is a statement in BASIC.

```
10 PRINT "WHICH WOULD YOU LIKE, A DAISY OR A DANDELION?"
20 INPUT C$
30 IF C$ = "DAISY" THEN PRINT "YOU CHOSE A FLOWER."
40 IF C$ = "DANDELION" THEN PRINT "YOU CHOSE A WEED."
```

Line 30 contains an IF-THEN statement. These two words are used in one line of a program. Line 30 tells the computer that *IF* the user stores DAISY in C$, *THEN* it should print YOU CHOSE A FLOWER. What if the user does not store DAISY in C$? Then the computer *ignores* line 30. It passes right over it and goes on to line 40. Line 40 tells the computer that *IF* the user stores DANDELION in C$, *THEN* it should print YOU CHOSE A WEED.

Here is the output of the program when the user answers DAISY:

```
WHICH WOULD YOU LIKE, A DAISY OR A DANDELION?
?DAISY
YOU CHOSE A FLOWER.
```

Here is the output when the user answers DANDELION:

```
WHICH WOULD YOU LIKE, A DAISY OR A DANDELION?
?DANDELION
YOU CHOSE A WEED.
```

Suppose the user decides to type ROSE. Here is the output:

```
WHICH WOULD YOU LIKE, A DAISY OR A DANDELION?
?ROSE
```

The computer printed *nothing* else in the output. Why? Line 30 says IF C$ = "DAISY" THEN PRINT "YOU CHOSE A FLOWER." But, the user answered ROSE, so C$ is ROSE. The computer *ignores* line 30 and moves on to line 40. Line 40 says IF C$ = "DANDELION" THEN PRINT "YOU CHOSE A WEED." Is C$ DANDELION? No, C$ is still ROSE, so the computer *ignores* line 40 and moves to line 50 which is END. The computer reaches line 50 without printing any further message.

Here is a program that uses two symbols you have probably used in math:

> is greater than

< is less than

Do not use the words *is* **or** *than* **with these symbols.**

Look at the program and part of the output.

```
10 PRINT "HOW OLD ARE YOU?"
20 INPUT A
30 IF A = 18 THEN PRINT "YOU ARE OLD ENOUGH TO VOTE."
40 IF A > 18 THEN PRINT "YOU ARE OLD ENOUGH TO VOTE."
50 IF A < 18 THEN PRINT "YOU ARE NOT OLD ENOUGH TO VOTE."
RUN
HOW OLD ARE YOU?
?
```

Suppose the user types 17 for the response. 17 is stored in address location A. Then the computer will pass over line 30 (A does *not* equal 18). It will pass over line 40 (A is *not* greater than 18). But, it will "read" line 50 because A *is* less than 18. The output will be:

```
HOW OLD ARE YOU?
?17
YOU ARE NOT OLD ENOUGH TO VOTE.
```

THE COMPUTER IGNORED LINES 30 AND 40.

If the user answers 22, the output will be:

```
HOW OLD ARE YOU?
?22
YOU ARE OLD ENOUGH TO VOTE.
```

If the user answers 18, the output will be:

```
HOW OLD ARE YOU?
?18
YOU ARE OLD ENOUGH TO VOTE.
```

There is a shortcut in BASIC that allows you to combine line 30 and 40 into one line by combining the symbols $>$ and $=$.

You can also reverse the symbols like this: $=>$

```
IF A >= 18 THEN PRINT "YOU ARE OLD ENOUGH TO VOTE."
```

This line tells the computer that *if A is greater than or equal to 18*, then it is to print "you are old enough to vote."

You can use IF-THEN statements to write a computer quiz. But, be careful. Remember, the computer is a "dumb" machine. It does not know the answers to any questions. So, when you start to program a computer quiz, you must not only choose the question, you must know the answer as well. You must also choose a question that has only *one* correct answer. Here's an example.

```
10 PRINT "HOW MANY STATES ARE IN THE U.S.?"
20 INPUT S
30 IF S = 50 THEN GOTO 60
40 IF S > 50 THEN PRINT "NO, TRY AGAIN."
45 IF S < 50 THEN PRINT "NO, TRY AGAIN."
50 GOTO 20
60 PRINT "THAT'S RIGHT!"
```

Let's trace the program:

Line 10 prints the question on the screen.

Line 20 allows the user to type in a response. The response is stored in the S address location.

Line 30 tells the computer that if S is 50, then jump to line 60 which prints THAT'S RIGHT! Then, the computer goes to line 70, and the quiz is over. But, if S does *not* equal 50, then the computer will ignore line 30 and go on to line 40.

Line 40 tells the computer that if S is greater than 50, it is to print NO, TRY AGAIN. If S is *not* greater than 50, then the computer will ignore line 40 and go on to the next line.

Line 45 tells the computer that if S is less than 50, it is to print NO, TRY AGAIN.

Line 50 tells the computer to go back to line 20 so the user can type in another answer. That answer will be stored in S, replacing the old answer.

As you can see, the computer cannot get to line 60 unless S equals 50.

You can use a shortcut to combine lines 40 and 45:

```
40 IF X < > 50 THEN PRINT "NO, TRY AGAIN."
```

There are two ways to read this line:

If S *is less than or greater than* 50, . . .
If S *does not equal* 50, . . .

Now the program stored in RAM looks like this:

```
10 PRINT "HOW MANY STATES ARE IN THE U.S.?"
20 INPUT S
30 IF S = 50 THEN GOTO 60
40 IF S < > 50 THEN PRINT "NO, TRY AGAIN."
50 GOTO 20
60 PRINT "THAT'S RIGHT!"
```

There is still another shortcut you can use in this program. Perhaps you have already thought of it yourself. Examine lines 30 and 40 closely. If S equals 50, then the computer will jump down to line 60. What if S does *not* equal 50? The computer ignores line 30 and goes on to line 40. The computer will go to line 40 *only if* S does *not* equal 50. So, there is no need to say IF S < > 50. You can change line 40 to:

```
40 PRINT "NO, TRY AGAIN."
```

Now the computer quiz, with all the shortcuts, looks like this:

```
10 PRINT "HOW MANY STATES ARE IN THE U.S.?"
20 INPUT S
30 IF S = 50 THEN GOTO 60
40 PRINT "NO, TRY AGAIN."
50 GOTO 20
60 PRINT "THAT'S RIGHT!"
```

Pretend you are running this program and you answer the question with 44, then 52, and finally 50. The entire output would look like this:

```
HOW MANY STATES ARE IN THE U.S.?
?44
NO, TRY AGAIN.
?52
NO, TRY AGAIN.
?50
THAT'S RIGHT!
```

This program can be made even shorter. You can put two statements on one line by using a **colon** (:). Look carefully at lines 30 and 40.

The *less than* and *greater than* signs are combined.

WHY ARE YOU ALWAYS TRYING TO MAKE PROGRAMS SHORTER?

GOOD PROGRAMMERS TRY TO SHORTEN THEIR PROGRAMS TO SAVE RAM SPACE.

```
10 PRINT "HOW MANY STATES ARE IN THE U.S.?"
20 INPUT S
30 IF S = 50 THEN PRINT "THAT'S RIGHT!": END
40 PRINT "NO, TRY AGAIN.": GOTO 20
```

In line 30, if S = 50, the computer will print THAT'S RIGHT! Then, the program will end. But, if S does *not* equal 50, the computer will ignore the entire line, including the END statement. When the computer gets to line 40 it will follow both instructions: PRINT "NO, TRY AGAIN." and GOTO 20.

Here is another kind of program that uses several statements you have learned. It prints the numbers from 1 to 100 in a column on the screen.

```
10 LET X = 1
20 PRINT X;
25 IF X = 100 THEN END
30 LET X = X+1
40 GOTO 20
RUN
1 2 3 4 5 6 7 8 ...
```

On your computer, the numbers may run together.

Line 10 stores a 1 in X.

Line 20 prints what is stored in X.

Without line 25, you would have an infinite loop!

Line 25 tells the computer to end if X equals 100. If X does *not* equal 100, the computer goes to the next line.

Line 30 adds 1 to the number stored in X.

Line 40 sends the computer back to line 20. The program keeps running until 100 is stored and printed.

1. Trace this program carefully and write the output.

```
10 LET P = 2
20 PRINT P
30 IF P = 20 THEN END
40 LET P = P+2
50 GOTO 20
```

2. Complete line 30 of this program so the computer will print the output shown.

```
10 Z = 5
20 PRINT Z;
30 IF
40 Z = Z+5
50 GOTO 20
RUN
5 10 15 20 25 30 35 40 45 50
```

On your computer the numbers may run together.

3. Write line 40 of this program so the computer will print the output shown.

```
10 F = 100
20 PRINT F;
30 IF F = 0 THEN END
40
50 GOTO 20
RUN
100 90 80 70 60 50 40 30 20 10 0
```

4. Write the output for this computer quiz. Make your first answer 4, your second answer 15, and your third answer 10.

```
10 PRINT "HOW MANY DIMES ARE IN ONE DOLLAR?"
20 INPUT D
30 IF D = 10 THEN PRINT "RIGHT!": END
40 IF D < 10 THEN PRINT "NOT ENOUGH—TRY AGAIN.": GOTO 20
50 IF D > 10 THEN PRINT "TOO MANY—TRY AGAIN.": GOTO 20
```

5. Write a computer quiz which asks, "What is the capital of South Dakota?"

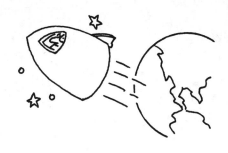

Remember the answer to this question is a *string*. Use a string address location and quotes around the string.

6. Write the output for the program you wrote in exercise 5. Pretend the user answers BISMARCK on the first try, and PIERRE on the second try.

THE CAPITAL OF SOUTH DAKOTA IS PIERRE.

At the Computer

1. Type and run this program:

```
10 LET W = 10
20 PRINT W
30 IF W = 1 THEN GOTO 60
40 LET W = W − 1
50 GOTO 20
60 PRINT "BLAST OFF!"
```

Line 40 subtracts 1 from the number in W each time the computer loops from line 50 to line 20.

Your output should be a column of numbers from 10 to 1 and the words BLAST OFF! Now add line 25 and run the program again:

```
25 IF W = 6 THEN PRINT "I AM HALFWAY THERE."
```

123

Type NEW to erase your ➡ old program.

2. Before you type and run this program, try to figure out what the output will be.

```
10 LET X = 10
20 PRINT X
30 IF X = 100 THEN END
40 LET X = X + 10
50 GOTO 20
```

The output is a column of numbers that starts with 10. 10 is the first number stored in address location X. The last number printed in the output is 100. That is because line 30 instructs the computer to END if X is 100. The numbers in the output increase by 10. You can see that line 40 tells the computer to add 10 to the number in X every time the computer "reads" that line.

3. Change lines 10, 30, and 40 to:

```
10 LET X = 100
30 IF X = 200 THEN END
40 LET X = X + 50
```

Remember, type LIST to ➡ list your program.

List your program so you can see the new lines in order. Run your program. Now what is the first number in the output? What is the last number?

4. Change line 40 to:

```
40 LET X = X + 3
```

Run the program. Hey! What's happening? Why isn't the program stopping? Line 30 tells the computer to end when X is 200. Oh, X is never 200! X starts at 100, then it's 103, 106, 109 . . . until it gets to 199, 202, 205 . . . Well, if X is never 200, then the computer will just ignore line 30 and the program will never end. Stop the program.

To stop the program ➡ press BREAK, STOP, or CTRL and C.

5. Tell the computer to stop the program by changing line 30 to:

```
30 IF X > 200 THEN END
```

Run the program. As soon as the computer stores a number greater than 200 and prints it, the program ends.

Remember, the symbol ➡ > means "is greater than."

6. Use an IF-THEN statement in a loop, so the computer prints the even numbers from 0 through 60 in a column.

Type NEW. ➡

Type NEW before ➡ starting this program.

7. Type this program:

```
10 PRINT "WHICH WOULD YOU RATHER PET, A CAMEL OR A CROCODILE?"
20 INPUT P$
30 IF P$ = "CAMEL" THEN GOTO 50
40 IF P$ = "CROCODILE" THEN GOTO 70
50 PRINT "YOU PICKED A MAMMAL!"
60 GOTO 80
70 PRINT "YOU PICKED A REPTILE!"
80 END
```

Don't put any extra spaces in the quotes in lines 30 and 40.

Atari computer users
should type:
5 DIM P$(15)

Run the program twice. Answer CAMEL one time, and CROCODILE the next time. Do you see how the IF-THEN statements in lines 30 and 40 determine the computer's response?

8. Run the program again, and answer ROBIN. What is the computer's response? YOU PICKED A MAMMAL. What! A bird is not a mammal. Why did the computer say that? The computer was just following your instructions. It ignored lines 30 and 40 because P$ did not store CAMEL, and P$ did not store CROCODILE. So, the computer moved on to the next line, line 50, which told it to print YOU PICKED A MAMMAL. Then the computer moved on to line 60 which told it to go to 80 and end. To fix this bug, add line 45 to the program:

```
45 GOTO 1Ø
```

Now run the program, and answer ROBIN again.

Type NEW.

9. Type this program:

```
1Ø PRINT "CHOOSE ANY NUMBER FROM 1 TO 99."
2Ø INPUT N
3Ø IF N < 1Ø THEN PRINT "YOUR NUMBER HAS 1 DIGIT."
4Ø IF N = > 1Ø THEN PRINT "YOUR NUMBER HAS 2 DIGITS."
```

Run the program several times, using different numbers for your response. What happens if you answer with 500? The computer prints YOUR NUMBER HAS 2 DIGITS! But, 500 has 3 digits. Look carefully at line 40. Line 40 tells the computer to print a message if N is greater than or equal to 10. 500 is greater than 10, so the computer printed YOUR NUMBER HAS 2 DIGITS.

10. You can improve your program by adding line 25.

```
25 IF N > 99 THEN PRINT "YOUR NUMBER IS TOO BIG!" : GOTO 1Ø
```

List your program and read it. Now run the program and try 500 for your answer.

Type NEW first.

Atari computer users
type:
5 DIM C$(20)

11. Type this computer quiz. It is like the one you wrote.

```
1Ø PRINT "WHAT IS THE CAPITAL OF SOUTH DAKOTA?"
2Ø INPUT C$
3Ø IF C$ = "PIERRE" THEN PRINT "YOU'RE SMART!" : END
4Ø PRINT "NO, TRY AGAIN."
5Ø GOTO 2Ø
```

Run the program and type a wrong answer first. Then type the correct answer.

12. Change line 50 to:

```
5Ø GOTO 1Ø
```

Run the program. Do you see what difference that change makes?

If you live in South Dakota, use another state and capital.

You might not have spaces between the numbers on your computer screen.

Run the program to make sure it works.

Type NEW.

13. Change lines 10 and 30 so that the quiz asks for the name of *your* state capital. Then run the program.

14. Type NEW. Write a program to produce this output:

```
1 2 3 4 5 6 7 8 9 10 TEN
11 12 13 14 15 16 17 18 19 20 TWENTY
21 22 23 24 25 26 27 28 29 30 THIRTY
31 32 33 34 35 36 37 38 39 40 FORTY
```

Hint—first write a program to print the numbers 1 to 40 across the screen. Then add four more IF-THEN statements after the *PRINT* statement:

```
IF X = 10 THEN PRINT "TEN"
IF X = 20 THEN PRINT "TWENTY"
IF X = 30 THEN PRINT "THIRTY"
IF X = 40 THEN PRINT "FORTY"
```

15. Write a computer quiz. Think of the question and the answer before you start typing. Remember, if the answer to the question is a string, use a string address location. If it's a number, use a number address location.

Chapter 20 | ROLLING THE DICE

At Your Desk

Imagine a hat filled with numbers from 1 to 100. Reach in and pull out a number. It could be a 6; it could be a 66; it could be a 32. It could be any number from 1 to 100. Put the number back and pick another one. It could be a 45 or a 99 or a 2. It could even be the same number you picked last time. In this chapter you will see how the computer can pick a number as if it were drawing a number out of a hat.

Look at this first line of a program:

```
10 LET N = RND(25)
```

Random means without any order or pattern.

You know that the LET statement means the computer is going to store something in the address location N. But what is it going to store? It will store RND(25). *RND* stands for *random*. RND(25) means the computer is going to randomly choose a number from 1 to 25. One is always the lowest number it can choose. The number in parentheses is the highest number it can choose. In this example, it could pick any number from 1 to 25.

To find out what number the computer picks, add line 20 to the program.

```
10 LET N = RND(25)
20 PRINT N
```

Here are some sample outputs from this program. You don't know ahead of time what number the computer is going to choose and store in N. Line 20 tells the computer to print whatever is stored in address location N.

When *you* run the program, you may get a different output.

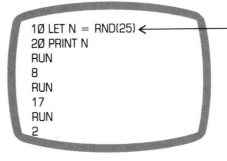

```
10 LET N = RND(25)
20 PRINT N
RUN
8
RUN
17
RUN
2
```

This is the highest number the computer can pick. The lowest number it can pick is 1.

127

Let's add a semicolon to line 20, and add line 30 so the program in RAM looks like this:

```
10 LET N = RND(25)
20 PRINT N;
30 GOTO 10
```

The program has an infinite loop. The program instructs the computer to pick a number from 1 to 25 and print it. Then, it sends the computer back to line 10. Again, the computer picks a number from 1 to 25 and prints it—and so on. Here is a sample output:

```
3 6 15 24 1 6 13 25 16...
```

If you were to run the program a few times, the output would look different each time.

Suppose you change line 10 so the program looks like this:

```
10 N = RND(3)
20 PRINT N;
30 GOTO 10
```

Now the computer can choose only numbers from 1 to 3. Here's what the output might look like:

```
1 2 1 3 3 1 2 2 1 1 3 3 3 1 2...
```

A special note for some computer users: Many computers do not generate random numbers as easily as you've seen so far. Many computers, including the Apple, Atari, and PET computers, choose random numbers differently.

In a statement such as

```
X = RND(8)
```

the number in parentheses is a "dummy" number. It has no special meaning. You could just as easily use:

```
X = RND(92)
```

Both of these statements give a decimal number between 0 and 1, which is stored in X. Look at this program and output.

```
10 X = RND(10)
20 PRINT X
30 GOTO 10
RUN
.2368392
.1479472
.3859285
```

Usually decimal numbers like these are not of much use. You need to turn them into whole numbers. Here is a way to do that:

Remember, an ⇨
infinite loop
goes on forever.

There might not be ⇨
spaces between the
numbers on your
computer.

If you are using a ⇨
TRS-80 computer, you
may skip this section.
Check with your teacher.

On your computer, the ⇨
numbers may be longer
or shorter than these.

When you multiply by 10, the decimal point moves one place to the right.

INT stands for **integer**. Integer means "whole number." INT is a statement in BASIC.

On the Apple computer, don't use 0 for a dummy number.

This section is for everyone.

For the Apple, Atari, and PET computers, lines 10 and 20 are:
D = INT(RND(1)*6)+1
E = INT(RND(1)*6)+1

10 N = RND(1)	Stores a decimal number in N, say .234967
20 N = N * 10	Multiplies N by 10; now N = 2.34967
30 N = INT(N)	N becomes the integer or *whole number* value of the new number. The numbers to the right of the decimal point are dropped, so now N = 2.
40 PRINT N	Prints 2
50 GOTO 10	Starts over again

```
RUN
2
9
3
6
.
.
.
```

This program will produce single digits, numbers from 0 to 9. What if you want numbers from 1 to 10? Just add 1 to N:

    35 N = N + 1

Here is a shortcut which combines lines 10, 20, 30, and 35:

    N = INT(RND(1) * 10) + 1

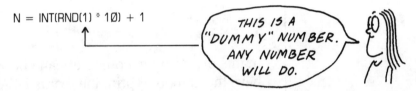

Use this statement when you want random numbers. The number after the multiplication sign should be the *highest* number you want. The number 1 will always be the lowest number. For example, if you want random numbers from 1 to 25, you would type:

    N = INT(RND(1) * 25) + 1

You can use the RND statement to have the computer "roll some dice."

```
10 D = RND(6)
20 E = RND(6)
30 PRINT "DIE #1 IS "; D
40 PRINT "DIE #2 IS "; E
```

WHY RND(6)?

BECAUSE DICE HAVE SIX NUMBERS TO CHOOSE FROM.

Now trace the program.

Line 10 tells the computer to pick some number from 1 to 6 and store it in D.

Line 20 tells the computer to pick some number from 1 to 6 and store it in E.

Line 30 tells the computer to print DIE #1 IS and the number stored in D.

Line 40 tells the computer to print DIE #2 IS and the number stored in E.

If you ran the program twice you might get this output.

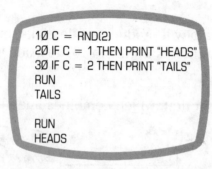

```
RUN
DIE #1 IS 5
DIE #2 IS 2

RUN
DIE #1 IS 4
DIE #2 IS 4
```

Remember, a computer simulation imitates a real-life situation.

For Apple, Atari, and PET computers, line 10 is:
C = INT(RND(1)*2) + 1

You can also use the RND statement to have the computer simulate tossing a coin. Take a look at this program.

```
10 C = RND(2)
20 IF C = 1 THEN PRINT "HEADS"
30 IF C = 2 THEN PRINT "TAILS"
RUN
TAILS

RUN
HEADS
```

In this program the computer can choose only 1 or 2. Lines 20 and 30 have the computer print the *words* HEADS or TAILS, not the random numbers.

Many programs for computer games use random numbers. Here's how to write a number guessing game. The computer will choose a number from 1 to 10 and the user has to guess it. Here are the first three lines:

```
10 N = RND(10)
20 PRINT "GUESS MY NUMBER FROM 1 TO 10."
30 INPUT G
```

For the Apple, Atari, and PET computers, line 10 is:
N = INT(RND(1)*10) + 1

A number from 1 to 10 is stored in N. A message is printed. Then the user makes a guess. The guess is stored in address location G. You have *two* address locations—N stores the computer's number; G stores the user's guess.

Next, you have to see if the user's guess is the same as the computer's number:

```
40 IF G = N THEN GOTO 70
50
60
70 PRINT "YOU GUESSED IT!"
```
We'll fill in these lines in a moment.

If the user's guess matches, a message is printed. But what if the guess is *not* the same as the computer's number? Then the computer will pass right over line 40 and go on to line 50:

```
50 PRINT "THAT'S NOT IT. TRY AGAIN."
60 GOTO 30
```

A message is printed and the user must guess another number. Now, put the program together.

```
10 N = RND(10)
20 PRINT "GUESS MY NUMBER FROM 1 TO 10."
30 INPUT G
40 IF G = N THEN GOTO 70
50 PRINT "THAT'S NOT IT. TRY AGAIN."
60 GOTO 30
70 PRINT "YOU GUESSED IT!"
```

Here is a sample output. Pretend that the computer is storing a 9 in address location N.

Computer's Number

User's Guesses

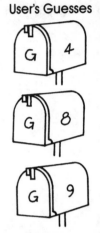

```
GUESS MY NUMBER FROM 1 to 10.
?4
THAT'S NOT IT. TRY AGAIN.
?8
THAT'S NOT IT. TRY AGAIN.
?9
YOU GUESSED IT!
```

1. Look at this program.

```
10 N = RND(20) ←——— For the Atari, Apple, and PET computers,
20 PRINT N              line 10 is:  N = INT(RND(1)*20) + 1
30 GOTO 10
```

  a. What is the greatest number the computer can choose?
  b. What is the least number the computer can choose?

2. Write a sample output for the program in exercise 1.

3. Write the two possible outputs for this program.

```
10 R = RND(2)
20 IF R = 1 THEN PRINT "RED"
30 IF R = 2 THEN PRINT "BLUE"
40 END
```

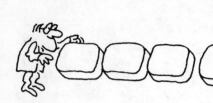

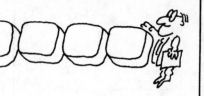

At the Computer

Apple, Atari, and PET
computer users type:
10 B = INT(RND(1)*12) + 1

1. Type and run this program:

   ```
   1Ø B = RND(12)
   2Ø PRINT B
   ```

   Run the program several times. You should always get a number from 1 to 12.

2. Add line 30:

   ```
   3Ø GOTO 1Ø
   ```

   Run the program. Are you getting one number after another, all from 1 to 12? Stop the program.

3. Change line 30 to:

   ```
   3Ø GOTO 2Ø
   ```

   Guess what's going to happen before you run the program. Notice that after the computer chooses a number (line 10) and prints it (line 20), it goes back to line 20 and prints the number again. It never goes back to line 10 to choose a new number. Now, run the program a few times. You won't know ahead of time what number the computer is going to pick, but, whatever number it is, the computer keeps printing it.

For Apple, Atari, and
PET computers, type:
10 F = INT(RND(1)*25) + 1

Your output should be
printed in zones.

4. Type NEW first. Then type this program:

   ```
   1Ø F = RND(25)
   2Ø PRINT F,
   3Ø IF F = 1Ø THEN END
   4Ø GOTO 1Ø
   ```

   Run it several times. Sometimes you get many numbers. Sometimes only a few. Why? The clue is in line 30. *If the computer stores and prints a 10, then* the program will end. It may take a long time for the computer to choose a 10, or it may not take long at all.

5. Change line 30 to:

   ```
   3Ø IF F = 5Ø THEN END
   ```

   Run the program. Will it ever stop? No! F can never be 50. The greatest number the computer can choose in this program is 25. Stop the program by yourself.

6. Type NEW. Then type this program. Run it a few times.

```
10 D = RND(6)
20 E = RND(6)
30 PRINT "YOUR ROLL IS:"
40 PRINT "DIE 1 "; D
50 PRINT "DIE 2 "; E
```

7. Add some lines to your program to roll four dice. Store random numbers in two more address locations, F and G. You'll need to use lines between 20 and 30. Use two more lines after line 50 to print the results of each roll.

8. Type NEW. Then type this computer math quiz. Run it a few times.

```
10 A = RND(40)
20 B = RND(20)
30 C = A + B
40 PRINT A; " + "; B; " = ";
50 INPUT X
60 IF X = C THEN GOTO 90
70 PRINT "TRY AGAIN."
80 GOTO 40
90 PRINT "RIGHT!"
```

For Apple, Atari, and PET computers, type:
10 A = INT(RND(1)*40) + 1
20 B = INT(RND(1)*40) + 1

Type line 40 very carefully.

9. Add line 100:

```
100 GOTO 10
```

Now the computer will continue to print new problems instead of ending. Run the program. Are the problems too easy? Change the random numbers in lines 20 and 30. You might try random numbers from 1 to 100. Then run the program again.

You have to stop the computer and list your program to change lines 20 and 30.

10. Try changing this program to a multiplication quiz. You'll have to change the addition sign in lines 30 and 40 to a multiplication sign (*). If the problems are too hard when you run the program, change the random numbers in lines 10 and 20.

11. It's time to play a number guessing game! Type NEW. Then type this program:

```
10 N = RND(10)
20 PRINT "GUESS MY NUMBER."
30 INPUT G
40 IF G = N THEN GOTO 70
50 PRINT "NO, TRY AGAIN."
60 GOTO 30
70 PRINT "YOU GUESSED IT!"
```

For Apple, Atari, and PET computers, type:
10 N = INT(RND(1)*10) + 1

Play the game (run the program) a few times.

12. Change line 10 to:

```
10 N = RND(100)
```

It could take a very long time to guess the right number. So, add some hints. Change line 50 to:

```
50 IF G > N THEN PRINT "TOO HIGH—TRY AGAIN."
```

Add this line:

```
55 IF G < N THEN PRINT "TOO LOW—TRY AGAIN."
```

Now run the program a few times.

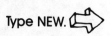
Type NEW.

13. Write a program to print random numbers from 1 to 99 in zones across the screen.

14. Change your program so that the computer prints random numbers from 1 to 9.

15. Add a line to your program so that the computer stops after it prints a 5.

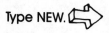
Type NEW.

16. Write a computer addition quiz. Program the computer to choose two numbers from 1 to 30 to add together. If the user gets the answer wrong, be sure the computer tells what the right answer is.

Type NEW.

17. Program a number guessing game. Have the computer choose a number from 1 to 500. Each time the user makes a guess, the computer should give a message such as TOO HIGH or TOO LOW.

Chapter 21 LOOPING AROUND

At Your Desk

You have used the statement GOTO to make a loop in a program. This program, for example, loops around and around and never ends:

```
10 PRINT "I'M LOOPING AROUND."
20 GOTO 10
```

This program is an example of an infinite loop.

In this chapter, you will learn how to tell the computer exactly how many loops you want it to make.

Look at this program.

```
10 FOR Z = 3 TO 9
20 PRINT Z
30 NEXT Z
```

FOR and NEXT are statements in BASIC.

It has two new statements—FOR and NEXT. They always appear as a pair in a program. If you have a FOR, you must have a NEXT. FOR and NEXT statements tell the computer how many loops to make. Let's trace the program.

Line 10 tells the computer to store a number in Z. But what number? The computer can store only one number at a time in an address location. It will start by putting the first number, 3, in address location Z. Then the computer will move to the next line.

Line 20 tells the computer to print whatever is in Z. So, it prints 3.

In line 30, NEXT Z means go back to the line with the FOR statement, and put the *next* number in address location Z.

So, the computer goes back to line 10 and puts the *next* number, 4, in Z.

Then the computer moves to line 20 and prints whatever is in Z, or 4.

Line 30 tells the computer to go back to the line with the FOR statement, line 10, and to put the *next* number, 5, in Z, and so on.

The computer continues to loop around from line 30 back to line 10 until all the numbers from 3 to 9 have been stored in Z. After 9

135

has been stored and printed, there are no more numbers to store in Z, so the program ends.

Here is the output for this program.

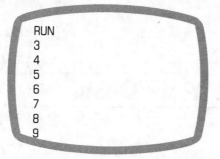

```
RUN
3
4
5
6
7
8
9
```

The program below has the computer print the numbers from 0 through 14 across the screen.

```
10 FOR H = Ø TO 14
20 PRINT H;
30 NEXT H
```

Suppose you want the computer to skip numbers instead of going to the *next* number in a loop. Look at how line 10 was changed in this program. Look at the output, too.

```
10 FOR H = Ø TO 14 STEP 2
20 PRINT H;
30 NEXT H
RUN
Ø  2  4  6  8  10  12  14
```

You can see from the output that STEP 2 tells the computer to count by two every time it goes back to line 10 and puts the next number in H. If the FOR statement does not say STEP at the end of the line, the computer automatically counts by one.

What do you think the output of this program will be?

```
10 FOR S = Ø TO 9 STEP 2
20 PRINT S;
30 NEXT S
40 END
```

The computer will print 0, 2, 4, 6, and 8. Then it will stop. It will never go beyond the second number in a FOR statement.

Here's another program using FOR-NEXT and STEP.

```
10 FOR V = 90 TO 80 STEP −1
20 PRINT V;
30 NEXT V
RUN
90  89  88  87  86  85  84  83  82  81  80
```

Negative numbers are numbers less than zero.

What's different about the STEP in this program? You can see that it is followed by a negative number. Look carefully at line 10. The numbers in the FOR statement go from 90 to 80. First, the computer prints 90. Then, STEP −1 causes the next number to be 89, then 88, and so on. To go from a larger number to a smaller number in a FOR-NEXT loop, you must always use STEP −1 (or −2 to go by twos, or −3 to go by threes, etc.).

Here is another program that uses a FOR-NEXT loop.

```
10 FOR J = 1 TO 3
20 PRINT "JUMP"
30 NEXT J
```

What do you think the output will be? You know that address location J will store the numbers from 1 to 3. But the program does not have a statement that prints J. Let's trace it.

Line 10 begins the loop by storing a 1 in J.
Line 20 instructs the computer to print JUMP.
Line 30 sends the computer back to line 10.
Now line 10 puts a 2 in J.
Line 20 prints JUMP again.
Line 30 sends the computer back to line 10.
Line 10 puts a 3 in J.
Line 20 prints JUMP again.
Line 30 sends the computer back to line 10. There are no more numbers to store, so the program ends.

Here is the program with its output.

```
10 FOR J = 1 TO 3
20 PRINT "JUMP"
30 NEXT J
RUN
JUMP
JUMP
JUMP
```

The computer program used the FOR-NEXT loop to count from 1 to 3. It printed JUMP for each number it counted.

Look at this program and its output.

Line 20 prints a number and a string.

```
10 FOR P = 1 TO 5
20 PRINT P; "KEEP GOING"
30 NEXT P
RUN
1 KEEP GOING
2 KEEP GOING
3 KEEP GOING
4 KEEP GOING
5 KEEP GOING
```

Look at line 20 carefully. Each time the computer goes through the loop, it prints the number stored in P. Then, on the same line it prints KEEP GOING. The first time through the loop, P is 1. So, the computer prints 1 KEEP GOING. The second time through the loop, P is 2. So the computer prints 2 KEEP GOING, and so on.

1. Write the output for this program.

```
10 FOR H = 13 TO 19
20 PRINT H
30 NEXT H
```

2. Write the output for this program.

```
10 FOR S = 3 TO 21 STEP 3
20 PRINT S
30 NEXT S
```

3. Find the bug in this program and fix it. Then write the output.

```
10 FOR C = 40 TO 35 STEP −1
20 PRINT C
30 END
```

4. Complete line 10 so the computer will print the output shown.

```
10
20 PRINT A;
30 NEXT A
RUN
7  9  11  13  15  17
```

At the Computer

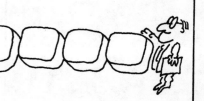

Using FOR-NEXT Loops

1. Type and run this program. Your output should be the numbers 2 through 12 in a column.

```
10 FOR B = 2 TO 12
20 PRINT B
30 NEXT B
```

Type NEW. ⇨

Line 20 tells the ⇨
computer to "print"
a space after each
number. (Some
computers
automatically put a
space between
numbers.)

Type NEW. ⇨

You can use your ⇨
name in line 20.

Type NEW. ⇨

Atari computer ⇨
users type:
2 DIM W$(20)

2. Add STEP 2 to line 10. Line 10 should look like this:

```
10 FOR B = 2 TO 12 STEP 2
```

Run the program. Your output should still begin with 2 and end with 12. But, it should step two numbers each time.

3. Type and run this program:

```
10 FOR Y = 100 TO 0 STEP −1
20 PRINT Y; " ";
30 NEXT Y
```

Don't forget the minus sign in STEP −1.

Did you get the numbers from 100 through 1 going across the screen?

4. Change line 10 to:

```
10 FOR Y = 100 TO 0 STEP −2
```

Run the program. Now make these changes and run the program after each change:

```
10 FOR Y = 100 TO 0 STEP −3
```

```
10 FOR Y = 100 TO 0 STEP −10
```

```
10 FOR Y = 100 TO 0 STEP −50
```

```
10 FOR Y = 100 TO 0 STEP −100
```

5. Type and run this program:

```
10 FOR U = 1 TO 10
20 PRINT "KAREN"
30 NEXT U
```

Did you get 10 Karens (or your name)?

6. What happens when you add STEP 2 to line 10?

```
10 FOR U = 1 TO 10 STEP 2
```

Try to figure out the output by tracing this program before you run it.

7. Type and run:

```
10 FOR L = 1 TO 5
20 PRINT "LOOPS"
30 NEXT L
```

You should have five LOOPS.

8. Change the program above by adding lines 3 and 5:

```
3 PRINT "TYPE ANY WORD."
5 INPUT W$
```

The users word is stored in W$.

Now change line 20 to:

```
20 PRINT W$
```

LIST your program. When you run the program and type a word, your word is stored in the W$ address location. When the computer goes through the FOR-NEXT loop and prints W$ (line 20), it will substitute your word for W$. Run the program a few times. Type in a different word each time.

9. Change line 20 to:

```
20 PRINT L; W$
```

Can you figure out the output before you run the program? Remember what is being stored in address location L. The first time through the loop, a 1 is stored. The next time through, a 2 is stored and so on.

10. Let's add two more lines to the program:

```
7 PRINT "TYPE A NUMBER."
9 INPUT N
```

The number the user types is stored here.

Now change line 10 to:

```
10 FOR L = 1 TO N
```

List your program. It should look like this:

```
3 PRINT "TYPE ANY WORD."
5 INPUT W$
7 PRINT "TYPE A NUMBER."
9 INPUT N
10 FOR L = 1 TO N
20 PRINT L,W$
30 NEXT L
40 END
```

WHAT IF I TYPE 632 ?

THE COMPUTER WILL READ: FOR L = 1 TO 632.

Run the program several times, responding with different words and different numbers.

11. Using a FOR-NEXT loop, write a program to print the numbers from 3 to 33 in a column.

12. Change a line in the program so the computer counts by threes. Your output should be 3 6 9 12 . . . 33, but, in a column.

13. Write a program to print the numbers starting with 99 and ending with 0. You decide how you want the output displayed on the screen.

14. Change a line in the program to print only the odd numbers.

15. Write a program to print I AM A TERRIFIC PROGRAMMER 10 times.

16. Change a line in the program to print I AM A TERRIFIC PROGRAMMER 100 times.

Remember, Atari computer users need a DIM statement in line 2.

Type NEW.

Type NEW.

Type NEW.

140

Time Delays

Type NEW before you begin.

If you forget how to stop the computer, look at page 95.

1. Type and run this program:

    ```
    10 PRINT "I NEVER STOP."
    20 GOTO 10
    ```

    OH- AN INFINITE LOOP AGAIN.

    Stop the computer. Then, add these lines and list the program.

    ```
    13 FOR P = 1 TO 500
    15 NEXT P
    ```

    Before you run the program, try to figure out what will happen. Lines 13 and 15 make a FOR-NEXT loop. The computer stores a 1 in address location P, then a 2, then a 3, and so on up to 500. What does the computer do after it stores a number in P? Nothing. It goes on to the *next* P and stores another number in P. The computer does not print anything from the time it stores one number in P to the time it stores the next number in P. But, it does take the computer some time to store all those numbers in P, one at a time.

    Run the program. You will see how long it takes the computer to store 500 numbers, one at a time, in address location P before it gets to line 20. Line 20 then sends it back to line 10. There is a pause after the computer prints each line of output. Stop the computer.

2. Change line 13 to:

    ```
    13 FOR P = 1 TO 1000
    ```

    Run the program. You can see that it takes the computer about twice as long to store 1000 numbers, one at a time, in address location P. Stop the computer.

3. Change line 13 to:

    ```
    13 FOR P = 1 TO 50
    ```

    Run the program. It does not take very long for the computer to store 50 numbers, one at a time, in address location P. Stop the computer.

4. Add these lines to your program:

    ```
    5 PRINT "CHOOSE ANY NUMBER. A HIGH NUMBER WILL MAKE THIS PROGRAM RUN
        SLOWLY. A LOW NUMBER WILL MAKE IT RUN FAST."
    7 INPUT N
    ```

    Now change line 13 to:

    ```
    13 FOR P = 1 TO N
    ```

    List your program. Then run it several times. Do you see why a high number slows down the output?

Remember, N is whatever number the user chooses.

Type NEW.

5. Write a program that prints SO LONG FOR NOW! over and over again, with a pause after each line or output.

At Your Desk

There are several ways of storing information in address locations. One way is to assign the information by using LET A = 2 or LET C$ = "COMPUTER." Another way is to ask for the information by using INPUT X or INPUT Z$. In this chapter, you will learn about a third way to store information.

Look at this program:

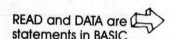

READ and DATA are statements in BASIC.

```
10 READ N
20 IF N = 0 THEN END
30 PRINT N
40 GOTO 10
50 DATA 1, 3, 5, 0
```

There are two new statements in this program—READ and DATA. They always go together in a program. If you have a READ statement, you must have a DATA statement, and vice versa.

When you have a lot of information, or data, to be used in a program, you can put that information in a DATA statement. The DATA statement in line 50 contains four numbers. Each piece of data is separated by a comma. Let's trace this program.

Line 10 says READ N. READ tells the computer to jump to the DATA statement, no matter where it is. The DATA statement can be at the beginning, middle, or end of the program. Wherever it is, the computer will find it. When the computer jumps to the DATA statement (line 50), it READs the first piece of data, the number 1. It stores the number 1 in address location N. Now the computer will continue with the line after the READ statement, line 20.

Line 20 tells the computer to end if N is 0. But, N is *not* 0, so the computer moves on to the next line.

Line 30 tells the computer to print the number stored in N, which is 1.

Line 40 tells the computer to go back to line 10 which is the READ statement.

Line 10 tells the computer to jump to the DATA statement. The computer never reads "old" data, so it will pass over 1. It will read the 3 and store it in N.

In line 20, the number stored in N is not 0. The computer moves on to line 30 and prints 3.

The computer goes back to line 10 and reads the next piece of data, the 5, and stores it in N. N is not 0, so the computer prints the 5.

The computer goes back to line 10 and reads the 0. When the computer gets to line 20, a 0 is stored in N, so the program ends.

Here is the program with its output.

```
10 READ N
20 IF N = 0 THEN END
30 PRINT N
40 GOTO 10
50 DATA 1, 3, 5, 0
RUN
1
3
5
```

The commas in line 50 ⇨ separate the pieces of data. They have nothing to do with zones.

The computer ended after it read the 0, but before it printed the 0. Zero is "dummy" data.

The computer can also read strings. In this program, each piece of data is stored in G$. STOP is the "dummy" data.

Atari computer users ⇨ need to use a DIM statement for G$.

```
10 READ G$
20 IF G$ = "STOP" THEN END
30 PRINT G$
40 GOTO 10
50 DATA BIKES, KEYS, SKATES, STOP
RUN
BIKES
KEYS
SKATES
```

WHAT! THE STRINGS IN THE DATA STATEMENT DON'T HAVE QUOTES AROUND THEM!

KEEP READING TO FIND OUT WHY!

The strings in line 50 do not have quotes around them. The DATA statement is one place where you do not have to put quotes around each string unless the string has a comma in it. For example, the string CLEVELAND, OHIO must be enclosed in quotes.

The computer can be instructed to READ more than one piece of DATA at a time. Look at line 10 in this program. The two address locations in the READ statement are separated by a comma.

Line 20 could also be: ⇨ IF D = 999 THEN END Both 999s are "dummy" data.

```
10 READ C, D
20 IF C = 999 THEN END
30 PRINT C, D
40 GOTO 10
50 DATA 5,2,8,12,6,10,999,999
```

WHY PUT TWO 999's AT THE END?

BECAUSE LINE 20 TELLS THE COMPUTER TO READ TWO PIECES OF DATA AT A TIME.

Line 10 instructs the computer to read *two* numbers, and store the first one in C and the second one in D. First, the computer will read 5

The comma in line 30 ⇨
separates the output
into two zones.

Atari computer users ⇨
need a DIM statement
for Z$.

STOP, 0, 0, 0 are ⇨
"dummy" data.

Be sure the strings
and numbers in
your DATA
statement match
up with the
addresses in your
read statement.

and 2. The next time through the loop, it will read 8 and 12. Then, it will read 6 and 10. The last time, it will read 999 and 999, and it will end. The output of the program looks like this:

```
5    2
8    12
6    10
```

The computer can read both numbers and strings. You must be sure the *strings* are stored in *string* address locations and *numbers* in *number* address locations. Here is an example:

```
10 READ Z$, A, B, C
20 IF Z$ = "STOP" THEN END
30 PRINT Z$, A, B, C
40 GOTO 10
50 DATA NORTH, 2, 7, 3, SOUTH, 2, 8, 4, EAST, 5, 2, 9,
   WEST, 6, 9, 1, STOP, 0, 0, 0
   RUN
   NORTH     2        7        3
   SOUTH     2        8        4
   EAST      5        2        9
   WEST      6        9        1
```

See how the string and number addresses in the READ statement match the string and numbers in the DATA statement:

```
10 READ Z$, A, B, C
        \  \ \ \
20 DATA NORTH, 2, 7, 3, . . .
```

The first time through the program, the computer READs NORTH and stores it in Z$; 2 and stores it in A; 7 and stores it in B; and 3 and stores it in C. When the computer gets to line 30, it prints NORTH 2 7 3 in zones. Then, it reads more data and prints it in four zones on the next line.

Let's change line 30 to do a calculation.

```
10 READ Z$, A, B, C
20 IF Z$ = "STOP" THEN END
30 PRINT Z$, A + B + C
40 GOTO 10
50 DATA NORTH, 2, 7, 3, SOUTH, 2, 8, 4, EAST, 5, 2, 9,
   WEST, 6, 9, 1, STOP, 0, 0, 0
   RUN
   NORTH     12
   SOUTH     14
   EAST      16
   WEST      16
```

This time, when the computer got to line 30, it printed the word stored in Z$ in the first zone, and the sum of the numbers stored in A, B, and C in the second zone.

If you know how many times you want the computer to READ information from the DATA statement, you do not need an IF-THEN statement to stop the computer from reading any more. You can use a FOR-NEXT loop instead. The following program has the computer

READ three pairs of numbers.

```
10 DATA 12, 5, 16, 4, 23, 7
20 FOR X = 1 TO 3
30 READ A, B
40 PRINT A; "+"; B; "="; A + B
50 NEXT X
RUN
12 + 5 = 17
16 + 4 = 20
23 + 7 = 30
```

FOR X = 1 TO 3?

YES -- THERE ARE 3 SETS OF DATA TO BE READ.

Each time the computer goes through the loop, it reads two numbers. It prints the numbers in an addition problem along with the sum of the numbers.

Many businesses use READ-DATA statements in their computer programs to calculate their employees' pay. Each person's name, the amount that person earns per hour, and the number of hours worked are the DATA for the program. The DATA statements in this program show this information for four employees. The program calculates and prints the total wages for each person. Read through the program carefully. The first number in each DATA statement is the hourly wage. The second number is the number of hours the person worked. The hourly wage is multiplied by the number of hours to get the total wages.

```
10 DATA BABBAGE, 6.87, 38
20 DATA ECKERT, 8.45, 41
30 DATA HOLLERITH, 12.06, 42
40 DATA JACQUARD, 9.22, 42
50 DATA END, −1, −1
80 PRINT "PAYROLL FOR THE A-Z COMPUTER CO."
90 PRINT "NAME", "TOTAL WAGES"
100 READ N$, W, H
110 IF W = −1 THEN END
120 PRINT N$, W * H
130 GOTO 100
RUN
PAYROLL FOR THE A-Z COMPUTER CO.
NAME          TOTAL WAGES
BABBAGE       261.06
ECKERT        346.45
HOLLERITH     506.52
JACQUARD      387.24
```

WHAT HAPPENED TO THE $? BABBAGE EARNS $6.87, NOT 6.87.

ADDING ANY OTHER SYMBOL WOULD MAKE 6.87 A STRING. YOU NEED A NUMBER TO CALCULATE THE TOTAL WAGES.

HMMM... THESE NAMES ARE FAMILIAR

The DATA statement ⇨ can go anywhere in the program.

You can put all the ⇨ data into one statement, or you can break it up into many statements. Look at lines 10-50 in the program.

No one's hourly wage ⇨ is −$1. So, −1 was used as "dummy" data.

1. Write the output for this program.

```
10 READ X
20 IF X = 99 THEN END
30 PRINT X
40 GOTO 10
50 DATA 2, 4, 6, 8, 10, 12, 99
```

Continued

2. Write the output for this program.

```
10 DATA HAPPY, SAD, SHORT, TALL, X, X
20 READ A$, B$
30 IF A$ = "X" THEN END
40 PRINT A$, B$
50 GOTO 20
```

3. Write the output for this program.

```
10 DATA SAM, 6, 2, SALLY, 10, 5, TOM, 9, 4
20 FOR X = 1 TO 3
30 READ A$, M, N
40 PRINT A$, M – N
50 NEXT X
```

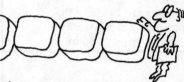

At the Computer

Now you're ready to put some DATA into the computer. But first, here is a bug alert for the whole section:

You may get a SYNTAX ERROR in a line with a READ statement, even though you typed the line correctly. The error may really be in a line with a DATA statement. For example, you may have put in an extra comma, or you may have forgotten a comma in the DATA line. So, the computer does not READ the information properly.

The opposite situation might also be true. A SYNTAX ERROR in a line with a DATA statement might mean the error is really in the line with the READ statement.

1. Type and run this program.

```
10 READ A$
20 IF A$ = "END" THEN END
30 PRINT A$
40 GOTO 10
50 DATA BATS, WORMS, FROGS, CENTIPEDES, END
```

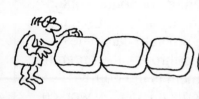

Atari computer users type:
5 DIM A$(15)

Your output should be four words in a column.

2. Type and run this program.

Type NEW.

```
10 FOR X = 1 TO 4
20 READ A, B, C
30 PRINT A + B + C
40 NEXT X
100 DATA 6, 3, 2
110 DATA 5, 5, 5
120 DATA 2, 1, 7
130 DATA 9, 4, 8
```

If you wish, combine these four statements into *one* line with a DATA statement.

3. Change line 30 to:

```
30 PRINT A; "+"; B; "+"; C; "="; A + B + C
```

Run the program again.

Type NEW.

Atari computer users type:
5 DIM N$(25)

If you have seven pieces of data, you need to loop around seven times.

Type NEW.

Atari computer users type:
5 DIM N$(20)

You are telling the computer to calculate and print the average of three numbers by adding them and dividing the sum by 3.

Type NEW.

Type NEW.

4. Type this program. Complete the DATA statement with the names of five of your favorite foods. Then run the program.

```
10 FOR X = 1 TO 5
20 READ N$
30 PRINT "I LIKE "; N$
40 NEXT X
100 DATA
```

5. Add another DATA statement to your program. Put in the names of two television shows. Then run the program. Did the television shows come out in the output? Why not? Look at line 10. How many loops do you want to make now? Change line 10, then run the program again.

6. Add another DATA statement with the name of your favorite sport. Remember to change line 10. Run the program.

7. This program prints the names of five students and their average grades for three tests. Type the program, filling in each DATA statement with a name and three test scores. There is an example in line 100. Run the program.

```
10 PRINT "NAME" , "AVERAGE SCORE"
20 PRINT "----" , "------- -----"
30 FOR X = 1 TO 5
40 READ N$, A, B, C
50 PRINT N$, (A + B + C)/3
60 NEXT X
100 DATA STACY, 94, 86, 89
110 DATA
120 DATA
130 DATA
140 DATA
```

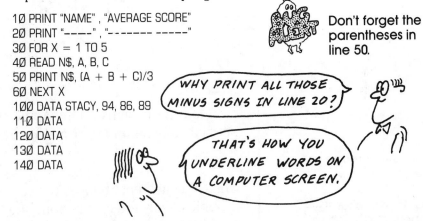

Don't forget the parentheses in line 50.

WHY PRINT ALL THOSE MINUS SIGNS IN LINE 20?

THAT'S HOW YOU UNDERLINE WORDS ON A COMPUTER SCREEN.

8. Below are members of the track team and their times for three races. Put this information in DATA statements. Then, print out a list of each student and his or her average time.

Wally	5.89	5.72	5.74
Liz	5.21	5.31	5.29
George	6.42	6.21	5.98
Rick	5.25	5.21	4.91
Kim	6.31	5.98	5.52

9. Use DATA statements to write the names of four friends, something they like, and something they dislike. For example, if Paul likes baseball and dislikes math, your DATA statement would be:

```
DATA PAUL, BASEBALL, MATH
```

Write a program to print a line for each friend, similar to this:

```
PAUL LIKES BASEBALL BUT DOESN'T LIKE MATH.
```

Chapter 23 | COMPUTER ART

Microcomputers can be programmed to draw designs. The designs are made up of blocks of light and, on some computers, colors and special shapes. A microcomputer's ability to display designs and graphs is referred to as computer **graphics**.

Each brand of computer must be programmed for graphics in its own way. This chapter is divided into four sections—each one for a different computer. Turn to the section for your computer: Apple computer, page 148; Atari computer, page 152; PET computer, page 160; TRS-80 computer, page 165.

The Apple Computer At Your Desk

To draw designs on the Apple computer, you need to use a special statement in your programs:

GR stands for **graphics**.

Text refers to letters, numbers, and symbols.

```
10 GR
```

The GR statement changes the screen so that it is ready to display graphics. Only the four bottom lines of the screen can be used for text. The rest of the screen is reserved for the picture that is being programmed.

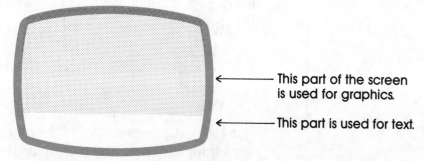

← This part of the screen is used for graphics.

← This part is used for text.

Now imagine that the top part of the computer screen is a graph with many small squares like the picture on the next page. The computer can be programmed to draw the spaceship on the screen by coloring in certain boxes to make a pattern.

Graphics Sheet for the Apple Computer

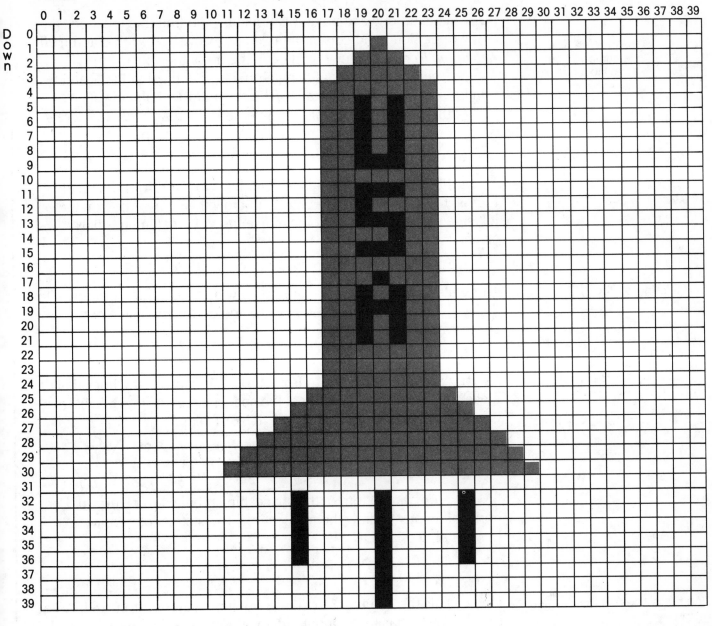

In order to color in a box on the screen, you need to choose a color. Your choices are:

0 black	6 medium blue	11 pink	
1 red	7 light blue	12 green	
2 dark blue	8 brown	13 yellow	
3 purple	9 orange	14 aqua	
4 dark green	10 grey	15 white	
5 grey			

The color black (0) is the background color of your screen. It will not show up unless it is used over another background color.

Suppose you wanted to color the tip of the spaceship green. You would use these statements:

```
COLOR = 12
PLOT 20, 1
```

The number for green is 12.

149

You can use only the numbers from 0 to 39 to locate a square.

PLOT lights up one square at location 20, 1. To find this location, start at the upper left-hand corner of the graph. Move *across* to column 20 and *down* to row 1. You should be at the tip of the spaceship.

You can color in any rectangle on the screen using PLOT and two numbers separated by a comma. The *first* number tells how far *across* the screen. The *second* number tells how far *down* the screen.

Now, choose the color red to fill in the spaceship.

    20 COLOR = 1

The Apple has two statements which allow you to draw horizontal (across) and vertical (down) lines. To draw the straight line on the left side of the spaceship, you can use the VLIN statement. VLIN stands for "vertical line."

    30 VLIN 4, 24 AT 17

Find this line on the graph.

SAME LINE, BUT DRAWN 23 SPACES ACROSS.

This statement tells the computer to draw a vertical line from row 4 to 24, at column 17. To draw the straight line on the right side of the spaceship you would type:

    40 VLIN 4, 24 AT 23

As you can see, both lines go from 4 to 24. In fact, all the lines that make up the rectangular body of the spaceship go from 4 to 24. They can all be drawn at once using a FOR-NEXT loop:

    30 FOR X = 17 TO 23
    40 VLIN 4, 24 AT X
    50 NEXT X

X KEEPS CHANGING. FIRST IT'S 17, THEN 18, THEN 19,... AND FINALLY, IT'S 23.

The top and bottom of the spaceship still need to be drawn. Use horizontal lines to draw the top section. The statement to draw a horizontal line is HLIN:

    60 HLIN 18, 22 AT 3
    70 HLIN 19, 21 AT 2

Find these lines on the graph.

Line 60 tells the computer to draw a line going across from 18 to 22 at row 3. Line 70 has the computer draw a horizontal line from 19 to 21 at row 2.

The top of the spaceship is one rectangle at location 20, 1. This statement (which you've seen before) colors the rectangle:

    80 PLOT 20, 1

Remember, the location is 20 across and 1 down.

The bottom section of the ship is left for you to do in "Try These."

Now, choose another color for the letters "USA."

    200 COLOR = 2

The main part of the ship will be red. When you color in the letters over the red, they will be dark blue.

At this point in the program, the computer will switch to dark blue. The letters can be programmed using VLIN, HLIN, and PLOT. This part of the program draws the letter "U":

    210 VLIN 5, 9 AT 19 ←———— Left side of the "U"
    220 VLIN 5, 9 AT 21 ←———— Right side of the "U"
    230 PLOT 20, 9 ←———— Bottom of the "U"

You will be asked to program the other letters in "Try These."

Don't forget to use the statements you used in exercises 1 and 2.

You may want to choose a different color for each initial.

1. What is the statement that instructs the computer to clear the screen for graphics?

2. What statement would you use to draw in dark green?

3. Write a program to light up a square in each of the four corners of the screen.

4. Write a program to draw a horizontal line across the top of the screen and a vertical line down the middle of the screen. The two lines will look like a large letter "T." (Choose a color for the lines.)

5. Draw your initials on a graphics sheet. Then, write a program to draw them on the computer. If there are any curves, such as in the letter C, you will have to use straight or diagonal lines. Your letters can be any size and any color.

6. Write a program to fill the entire graphics screen with a color of your choice. You can use either horizontal or vertical lines.

7. Write a program to draw the base of the spaceship on page 149.

8. Write a program for the flames coming out of the spaceship.

9. Write a program for the letters "S" and "A" in "USA."

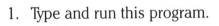

At the Computer

1. Type and run this program.

```
10 GR
20 COLOR = 3
30 H = INT(RND(1)*40)
40 V = INT(RND(1)*40)
50 PLOT H, V
60 GOTO 20
```

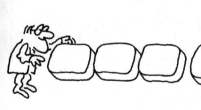

HMMM-- LINES 30 AND 40 ARE CHOOSING NUMBERS FROM 0 TO 39.

THOSE ARE THE NUMBERS ALONG THE EDGES OF THE GRAPHICS SHEET!

2. Stop the computer and list the program. You can't read all the lines because they roll off the top of the text screen. To change the whole screen back to text, type the command:

TEXT

You can clear the screen by typing HOME.

Now, the color can be any number from 1 to 15.

Type NEW.

The graphics screen will change to text. Now you can list your program. Change line 20 to:

```
20 COLOR = INT(RND(1)*15)+1
```

WOW, LOOK AT THAT COLORFUL OUTPUT!

Run the program again.

3. Draw a square that "moves" across the screen.

```
10 GR
20 FOR H = 0 TO 39
30 COLOR = 9
40 PLOT H, 20
50 COLOR = 0
60 PLOT H, 20
70 NEXT H
80 GOTO 20
```

As you can see, the square is not really moving. You are coloring in one square, then erasing it by coloring it black (the background color). Then, you are coloring in the next square, erasing it, and so on.

Type NEW.
Type NEW.

4. Draw a square that "moves" down the screen.

5. Type and run a program to draw your initials. Use your program from "Try These" exercise 5.

Don't use numbers larger than 39, or you'll get an error message!

Type NEW.

6. Draw the entire spaceship shown on page 149. You have already done part of the work in "At Your Desk." Use whatever colors you like. You may wish to begin by programming a background color over the entire screen.

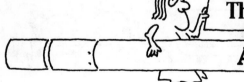

The Atari Computer

At Your Desk

To draw pictures on the Atari computer, you need to use a special statement in your programs:

```
GRAPHICS 3 (or GR. 3)
```

On older models there may be fewer numbers that you can use.

There are eleven numbers, 0 to 10, that you can use with the GRAPHICS statement. For now, you will use only GRAPHICS 3.

The GRAPHICS 3 statement changes the screen so that it is ready to display graphics. Only the four bottom lines of the screen can be

Text refers to letters, numbers, and symbols.

used for text. The rest of the screen is reserved for the picture that is being programmed.

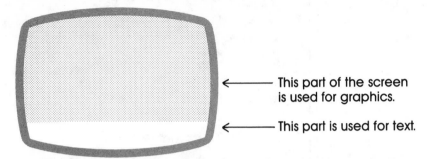

← This part of the screen is used for graphics.

← This part is used for text.

Imagine that the top part of the screen is a graph with many small squares like the picture on the next page. The computer can be programmed to draw pictures on the graphics screen by coloring in a pattern of squares.

In order to see anything on the screen, you must tell the computer you want to use colors by typing:

COLOR 1

YOU CAN USE SOME OTHER NUMBER AFTER THE <u>COLOR</u> STATEMENT.

YES, BUT YOU DON'T USE 0 FOR NOW. IT IS THE BACKGROUND COLOR. YOUR GRAPHICS WON'T SHOW UP ON THE SCREEN.

The statement that is used for lighting up one square on the screen is PLOT. To plot a square, you have to identify it with two numbers like this:

PLOT 19, 13

This statement lights up one square at location 19, 13. To find this location, start at the upper left-hand corner of the graph. Move *across* to column 19 and *down* to row 13. You will see that this is the top of the letter "A" on the spaceship.

You can color in any square on the screen using PLOT and two numbers separated by a comma. The *first* number tells how far *across* the screen. The *second* number tells how far *down*.

You might be thinking that it would take a very long time to "plot" squares to draw a picture. But the Atari computer uses a statement that can do a lot of work for you. Look at this program:

```
10 GR. 3 ←————————— Set up the screen for graphics.
20 COLOR 1 ←————————— Use color.
30 PLOT 0, 0 ←————————— Draw a square at 0 across and 0 down.
40 DRAWTO 5, 5 ←————————— A new statement!
```

Find these squares on the graph.

DRAWTO in line 40 means "draw a line to." So, the computer will plot a square at 0, 0 and then draw a line from that position to position 5, 5.

The output is a diagonal line like this:

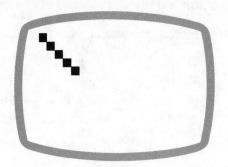

Here's a program for part of the spaceship colored in on the graph. It uses COLOR, PLOT, and DRAWTO:

```
10 GR. 3
20 COLOR 1
30 PLOT 17, 2: DRAWTO 17, 13 ⎤
40 PLOT 18, 1: DRAWTO 18, 13 │
50 PLOT 19, 0: DRAWTO 19, 13 │     These lines draw the
60 PLOT 20, 1: DRAWTO 20, 13 │     "tall" part of the
70 PLOT 21, 2: DRAWTO 21, 13 ⎦     spaceship.
80 PLOT 16, 14: DRAWTO 22, 14 ⎤
90 PLOT 15, 15: DRAWTO 23, 15 │    These lines draw the
100 PLOT 14, 16: DRAWTO 24, 16 ⎦   bottom of the spaceship.
```

Find these squares and lines on the graph.

Remember, use a colon when you have two statements on one line.

If you don't tell the computer what colors to use, it will choose the colors for you. It will choose black for the graphics background, blue for the text background, and orange for the graphics squares. To choose your own colors, you must use a new statement—SETCOLOR—along with COLOR.

Across

Atari Graphics Sheet for GRAPHICS 3

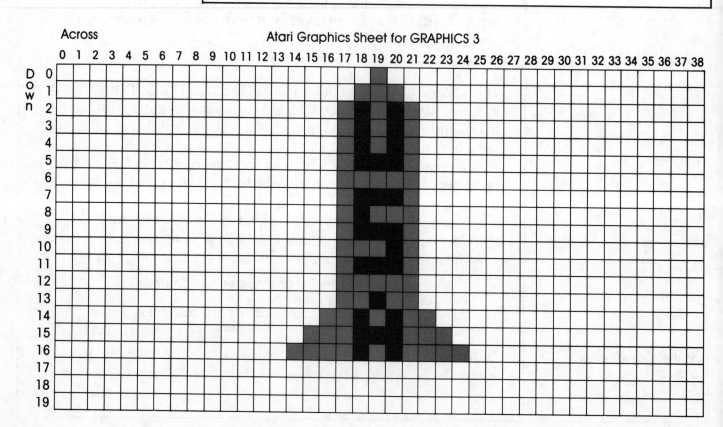

SETCOLOR means you are going to "set" or choose a color. SETCOLOR is followed by three numbers such as these:

SETCOLOR Ø, 12, 2

Let's look at one number at a time. The first number chooses *what* you want to color. It is called the color register. In GRAPHICS 3, you can use the numbers 0, 1, 2, or 4:

0 and 1 mean choose a color for the graphics squares.
2 means choose a color for the text background.
4 means choose a color for the graphics background.

You can't use the number 3 when you are in GRAPHICS 3.

The color register in SETCOLOR 0, 12, 2 is 0. It tells the computer you will be choosing a color for the graphics squares.

The second number chooses the color. You can use the numbers 0-15:

0 grey	6 lavender	11 green-blue
1 gold	7 blue	12 green
2 orange	8 blue	13 yellow-green
3 red-orange	9 light blue	14 orange-green
4 pink	10 turquoise	15 light orange
5 purple		

The second number in the SETCOLOR statement above is 12, so the statement tells the computer to choose the color green. So far, the SETCOLOR statement means the computer will color graphics squares green.

The third number chooses the brightness of the color. You can use the numbers 0 to 14. Zero is the brightest; fourteen is the darkest. The third number in the SETCOLOR statement above is 2, so the computer will draw very bright green squares.

Number 10 causes a blank screen. Don't use it!

SETCOLOR only *chooses* what you want to color (the color register, the color, and the brightness). To *put* the color on the screen you need to use the COLOR statement. COLOR is followed by 0, 1, 2, or 3. The number is *always* one more than the color register in SETCOLOR. (If the register number in SETCOLOR is 4, then the COLOR number is 0.) Here are some examples:

The color register is the first number after SETCOLOR.

```
SETCOLOR Ø, 12, 8          SETCOLOR 1, 7, 8
COLOR 1                    COLOR 2


SETCOLOR 2, 15, 8          SETCOLOR 4, 2, 8
COLOR 3                    COLOR Ø
```

Look back at page 154.

Now, you can choose colors for the spaceship program. These lines replace old lines 10 and 20.

```
10 GR. 3
12 SETCOLOR 4, 9, 14
14 COLOR Ø
16 SETCOLOR Ø, Ø, 12
18 COLOR 1
```

Line 12 chooses light blue for the graphics background. Line 14 puts the color on the screen. Line 16 chooses grey for the graphics squares which make up the spaceship. Line 18 puts the color on the screen.

Now, you're ready to draw the letter "U." First, you have to change the color. If you don't, the color will be the same as the spaceship, and the letter "U" won't show up.

You will be asked to program the other letters in "Try These."

```
100 SETCOLOR 1, 3, 2 ─┐
110 COLOR 2          ─┘ ──── Choose a color and bright-
                              ness for the graphics squares.
120 PLOT 18, 2: DRAWTO 18, 5 ─┐ Put the color on the screen.
130 PLOT 20, 2: DRAWTO 20, 5 ─┘ ──── Draw the "U."
140 PLOT 19, 5
```

Line 100 is very important. Remember, you can use 0 or 1 for the color register to choose a color and brightness for graphics squares. You already used 0 in line 16. If you use 0 again, the computer would change *all* the graphics squares to the new color. Since you want the letter "U" to be a different color, you must use a different color register (1) for those squares.

The four color registers, 0, 1, 2, and 4, allow you to have four different colors on the screen at one time. In the spaceship program, the graphics squares (registers 0 and 1) are grey and red-orange. The graphics background (register 4) is light blue. No color was chosen for the text background, so it is automatically blue.

So far you have seen only GRAPHICS 3. GRAPHICS 4, 5, 6, 7, 8, 9, and 10 work just like GRAPHICS 3, but they have more (and smaller) squares on the graphics screen. Some of the graphics numbers use other color registers than the ones that are used in GRAPHICS 3.

GRAPHICS 0 is used for text. The computer is automatically set in GR. 0 when you turn it on. You were using GRAPHICS 0 when you typed the programs in the other chapters in this book.

Your Atari computer manual has charts to show you which color registers to use. You can also experiment.

You can also use GR. 0 to clear the screen.

GRAPHICS 1 and GRAPHICS 2 are special. They allow you to write **graphics text**. Graphics text is letters, numbers, and symbols that are displayed on the graphics screen. They are made up of small graphics squares. Here is a program that prints graphics text in GRAPHICS 1 and regular text on the text screen.

A COLOR statement is not necessary with GR. 1 or GR. 2.

```
10 GR. 1
20 PRINT "THIS IS TEXT."
30 PRINT #6; "THIS IS GRAPHICS TEXT"
```

In line 30, PRINT #6; tells the computer to print in graphics text. The output of the program looks like this:

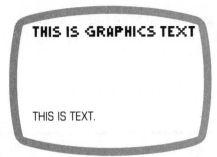

THIS IS GRAPHICS TEXT

THIS IS TEXT.

GRAPHICS 2 is the same, only the letters are taller.

1. Here are three graphics statements: GR. 0, GR. 1, GR. 3.

   a. Which statement is used for graphics screen display?

   b. Which statement is used for graphics text?

   c. Which statement is used for text only?

2. Name the statement that:

   a. chooses a color register, a color, and a brightness.

   b. tells the computer to draw with the chosen color and brightness.

   c. draws one square.

   d. draw a line.

3. The program below draws one square near the middle of the screen:

   ```
   10 GR. 3
   20 SETCOLOR
   30 COLOR
   40 SETCOLOR
   50 COLOR
   60 PLOT 19, 10
   ```

   a. Write lines 20 and 30 to make the background color light orange. (Choose any brightness you want.)

   b. Write lines 40 and 50 to make the square blue. (Any brightness will be all right.)

4. Write a program to light up a square in each of the four corners of the screen.

Continued

Choose a color for the graphics squares.

5. Write a program to draw a line across the top and a line down the right side of the screen.

6. Using graphics text, write a program to print your name on the graphics screen. (Remember, PRINT #6; is the statement for graphics text.)

7. Write a program to draw the letters "S" and "A" on the spaceship.

There are only two numbers you can use for graphics text.

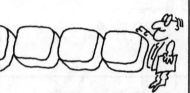

At the Computer

1. Type and run this program. Use your name in line 120.

   ```
   10 GR. 3
   30 COLOR 1
   70 PLOT 0, 0
   120 PRINT "GRAPHICS BY MARK MORRIS"
   ```

   You should see an orange square in the upper left corner of the screen. The graphics background is black, and the text background at the bottom of the screen is blue. GRAPHICS BY (your name) appears in the text screen.

2. Add another statement to line 70. If you start typing now, your new line 70 will be displayed in the text portion of the screen. Type:

   ```
   70 PLOT 0, 0: DRAWTO 19, 19
   ```

   Don't forget the colon.

   You can also press ⇨ SYSTEM RESET.

   Try to LIST your program. Part of it rolls off the top of the text screen. Clear the screen of graphics by typing GR. 0 (no line number). Now, you can list your program on the regular text screen. Run the program. You should see a diagonal line.

3. Type GR. 0 and list the program. Add this line:

   ```
   20 SETCOLOR 4, 5, 8
   ```

   Change line 30 to:

   ```
   30 COLOR 0
   ```

   RUN the program. You have changed the background color of the graphics screen. Retype line 20 several times, changing the color and brightness of the line. (But leave the color register, the first number, 4. We want to change only the background color.)

4. Add these lines:

```
100 SETCOLOR 2, 14, 8
110 COLOR 3
```

You are changing the color of the text background. Change the numbers for color and brightness several times.

5. Change the color of the diagonal line. Add these lines to your program:

```
50 SETCOLOR 0, 12, 2
60 COLOR 1
```

Run the program.

6. You can use a FOR-NEXT loop to change the line to all the colors. Add these lines:

```
40 FOR C = 0 TO 15
90 NEXT C
```

Change line 50 to:

```
50 SETCOLOR 0, C, 8
```

WOW! LOOK AT THAT COLORFUL OUTPUT!

RUN the program and watch the colors change. Does it run too fast? Put in a pause after you draw the line. Add:

```
80 FOR P = 1 TO 200: NEXT P
```

Run the program again.

Type NEW.

7. Draw a square that "moves" across the screen.

```
10 GR. 3
20 FOR A = 0 TO 38
30 SETCOLOR 0, 4, 6
40 COLOR 1
50 PLOT A, 10
60 COLOR 0 ←——————— COLOR 0 without SETCOLOR changes
70 PLOT A, 10              the graphics squares to the background
80 NEXT A                  color, "erasing" them.
```

Run the program. Of course, nothing is really moving. The computer PLOTted a square, "erased" it, then PLOTted a square in the next space, "erased" it, and so on.

8. Draw a square that "moves" down the screen.

9. Draw the entire spaceship shown on the graphics sheet. Part of the program appears in "At Your Desk." You have written the rest of the program in "Try These." Choose your own colors for the background, the spaceship, and the letters. Print a message in the text window, such as PROGRAMMED BY (your name).

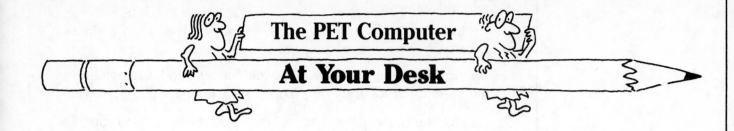

Imagine that the computer screen is a graph with many small squares like the picture on the next page. The PET computer can be programmed to draw pictures by filling in certain squares with graphics characters. Graphics characters are symbols, or little pictures. You can find them on the fronts of the keys on the keyboard. To print these characters on the screen, you must use the SHIFT key. For example, to print a diamond, you would hold down the SHIFT key and press Z.

Suppose you wanted to fill in one graphics square with a circle like the one in the upper left corner of the graphics sheet. First, you must be sure the cursor is at the top of the screen. To do this, you can clear the screen by using this statement:

10 PRINT "♡"

An **inverse heart** has the colors reversed. A black heart appears on a green background.

To type the heart, you press the CLR key as you are typing. You will see an **inverse heart** symbol appear on the screen.

You have already used the CLR key to clear the screen. By typing it in a PRINT statement as part of your program, you instruct the computer to clear the screen when you run the program.

The second line of the program is:

20 PRINT "●" ◀───────── To type the circle, you press SHIFT and Q.

Find the circle on the graph.

When you run the program, the circle appears at the beginning of the first line.

Look at the graph. The numbers go across from 0 to 39 and down from 1 to 25. Suppose you wanted to put the circle in the upper right-hand corner of the screen. You could put 39 spaces inside the quotes.

20 PRINT "   ●"   40th space—
you have to
count the zero.

You don't have to count spaces.

But, there is a shortcut that uses a new statement—TAB. This statement has the computer print the circle at box 39:

20 PRINT TAB(39) "●"

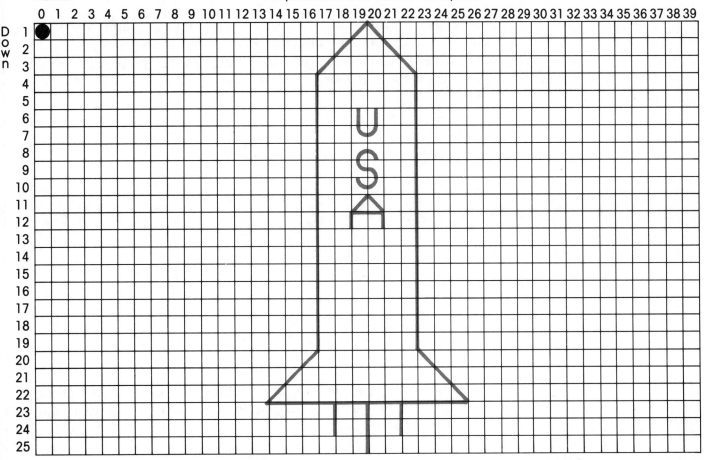

Look at the program and the output below. The program clears the screen and uses TAB statements to print symbols.

```
10 PRINT "♥"
20 PRINT TAB(5) "♥" TAB(10) "♦" TAB(15) "♣" TAB(20) "♠"
```

The heart in line 20 is ⇨ the regular heart. It is typed by pressing SHIFT and S.

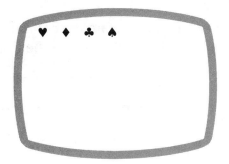

Suppose you want to print a graphics character farther down the screen. You can use the PRINT statement to do that. Using PRINT alone tells the computer to print a blank line. This program tells the computer to print a diamond 5 lines down, at box 9 (across):

Find this box on the ⇨ graph.

```
10 PRINT "♥"
20 PRINT: PRINT: PRINT: PRINT   ◄————— 4 lines of blanks
30 PRINT TAB(9) "♦"
```

There are 25 lines on the screen, so if you wanted a graphics character at the bottom of the screen, you would have to type 24 blank lines or 24 PRINTs. But you know a shortcut to take care of that—the FOR-NEXT loop:

```
10 PRINT "▨"
20 FOR X = 1 TO 24
30 PRINT
40 NEXT X
50 PRINT TAB(20) "○"
```

24 lines
of blanks

Here is the output:

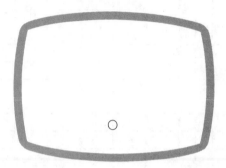

You can put together as many graphics characters as you want, to make a design. Here is a program to draw the top of the spaceship on the graph:

```
10 PRINT "▨"
20 PRINT TAB(19) "/\"
30 PRINT TAB(18) "/  \"
40 PRINT TAB(17) "/    \"
```

Look at the graph to find the output of lines 20, 30, and 40.

To draw the body of the spaceship you can use a FOR-NEXT loop. This part of the program draws two lines going down from 4 to 19:

```
50 FOR X = 4 TO 19
60 PRINT TAB(17) "|        |"
70 NEXT X
```

Since there are 16 lines of the pattern, you could also type:
50 FOR X = 1 TO 16

You will be asked to program the bottom of the spaceship in "Try These" and the letters "USA" in "At the Computer."

Use TABs and PRINTs to help you put the designs in the right positions.

1. When you type a graphics character, what additional key must you press?

2. Draw a design on a graphics sheet using any of the graphics characters you saw in this section. Write a program to draw the design on the screen.

3. Continue the spaceship program so it draws the bottom of the spaceship. Start with line 80.

4. Continue the spaceship so it draws the flames coming out of the bottom of the spaceship.

At the Computer

1. Practice typing several graphics characters. Remember to hold down the SHIFT key. You can also press the SHIFT/LOCK key until it clicks. It will keep the keyboard in the shift position. To get out of the shift position, press the SHIFT/LOCK key again.

2. The PET computer will draw a graphics character wherever the cursor is. It is important to know how to move the cursor around when you write a program. First, practice clearing the screen. Type:

It is good practice to clear the screen at the beginning of every program.

```
10 PRINT "♥"
```
Press CLR to get the heart. Don't forget the quotes.

RUN the program. Notice that the screen is cleared, and the cursor is in the top left-hand corner.

3. Now type:

Remember, a colon lets you put more than one statement on a line.

```
20 PRINT: PRINT: PRINT
30 PRINT "○"
```
Type SHIFT-W.

Run the program. You will see three blank lines and the circle on the fourth line.

4. There is another way to move the cursor down. You can use a PRINT statement, quotes, and the CRSR↓ key. Pressing the CRSR↓ key (inside the quotes) puts an inverse Q on the screen. Type these lines:

Remember, an inverse character is black on a green background.

```
40 PRINT "▯ ▯ ▯"
50 PRINT "●"
```

Run the program. You will see three blank lines, then a solid circle.

5. Now print a diamond *above* the circle. This time, you must use the CRSR↑ key in quotes. Pressing the CRSR↑ key (inside the quotes) puts an inverse dot on the screen. Type:

You can combine symbols in one statement.

```
60 PRINT "▯ ◆ "
```
This is the graphics diamond (SHIFT-Z).
↑ This is the CRSR ↑ key.

Now run the program.

Remember, the inverse
Q is typed by pressing
the CRSR↓ key.

6. You have already learned how to move the cursor to the right by using a TAB statement. Type:

    70 PRINT "◙ ◙ ◙ ◙ ◙" TAB(10) "♠"

    Line 70 will move the cursor down 5 lines from the diamond and print the spade on the sixth line, at 10 across.

7. There is one more important cursor movement—moving the cursor to the **home** position. The home position is the upper left-hand corner of the screen. To move the cursor to the home position and print a heart on the screen, type this line:

    80 PRINT " ⬛ ♠"

    To get the inverse S, press the HOME key (inside the quotes) as you type. Now run the program.

8. LIST the program from #2. It should look like this:

    ```
    10 PRINT "♥"
    20 PRINT: PRINT: PRINT
    30 PRINT "○"
    40 PRINT "◙ ◙ ◙"
    50 PRINT "●"
    60 PRINT "□ ♦"
    70 PRINT "◙ ◙ ◙ ◙ ◙" TAB(10) "♠"
    80 PRINT "⬛ ♠"
    ```

    After you RUN the program, you'll see the READY message on the screen. When you create a picture with graphics characters, the READY message might get in the way of your picture. So eliminate the READY message by making your program *never end*. To do this, type:

    90 GOTO 90

    THIS IS A ONE-LINE INFINITE LOOP!

    RUN the program. Line 90 keeps the computer busy. The program will never end, and the READY message will not appear. Use a one-line infinite loop at the end of all your graphics programs.

9. Draw your initials on a graphics sheet. You may wish to use thin lines, thick lines, curved lines, blocks, triangles, etc. Then, write a program to draw the initials on the screen.

10. Program the entire spaceship on page 161, but without the letters "USA."

11. Now add the letters "USA." Use graphics characters to make up the letters. Hint: You may want to use HOME, CRSR↑, and CRSR↓ in this program.

Remember to press
STOP when you want to
start typing again.

Type NEW.

Type NEW.

Type NEW.

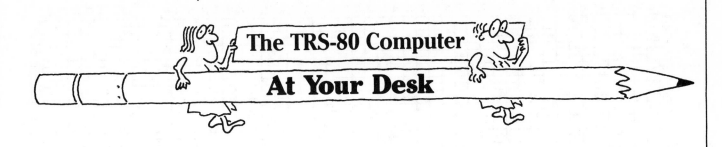

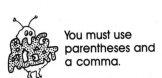

You must use parentheses and a comma.

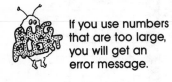

If you use numbers that are too large, you will get an error message.

Imagine that the computer screen is divided into many small boxes or rectangles like the graphics sheet on the next page. The computer can be programmed to draw a picture by lighting up certain rectangles to make a pattern. For example, a spaceship is represented by lighting up the rectangles shaded in on the graphics sheet.

The statement that is used for lighting up one rectangle on the screen is SET. This instruction lights up the rectangle that is the tip of the spaceship:

SET (62, 1)

To find the rectangle at location (62, 1), start at the upper left-hand corner of the graph. Move across to the column marked 62 and down to the row marked 1. You should be at the tip of the spaceship.

The first number in parentheses tells you how far *across* the screen. The *second* number tells you how far *down* the screen. This statement lights up the tip of the "A." Find it on the graph.

SET (62, 20)

Across   Down

You can light up any rectangle on the screen by using SET. But, you can use only the numbers on the graph. You can use numbers from 0 to 127 for the first number and numbers from 0 to 47 for the second number. For example, this statement lights up the rectangle in the upper right-hand corner of the screen:

SET (127, Ø)

You might be thinking that it would take a very long time to light all the rectangles to show the spaceship. You have learned other statements that can do a lot of the work for you. Look at this program:

```
1Ø FOR D = 7 TO 29
2Ø SET (56, D)
3Ø NEXT D
```

SET (56,D)?

YES, D REPRESENTS ALL THE BOXES GOING DOWN FROM 7 TO 29.

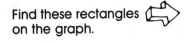

Find these rectangles on the graph.

This FOR-NEXT loop lets you light all the rectangles down the side of the spaceship with only one SET statement. These rectangles will light up, forming a vertical line: (56, 7), (56, 8), (56, 9), . . . (56, 29).

Graphics Sheet for the TRS-80

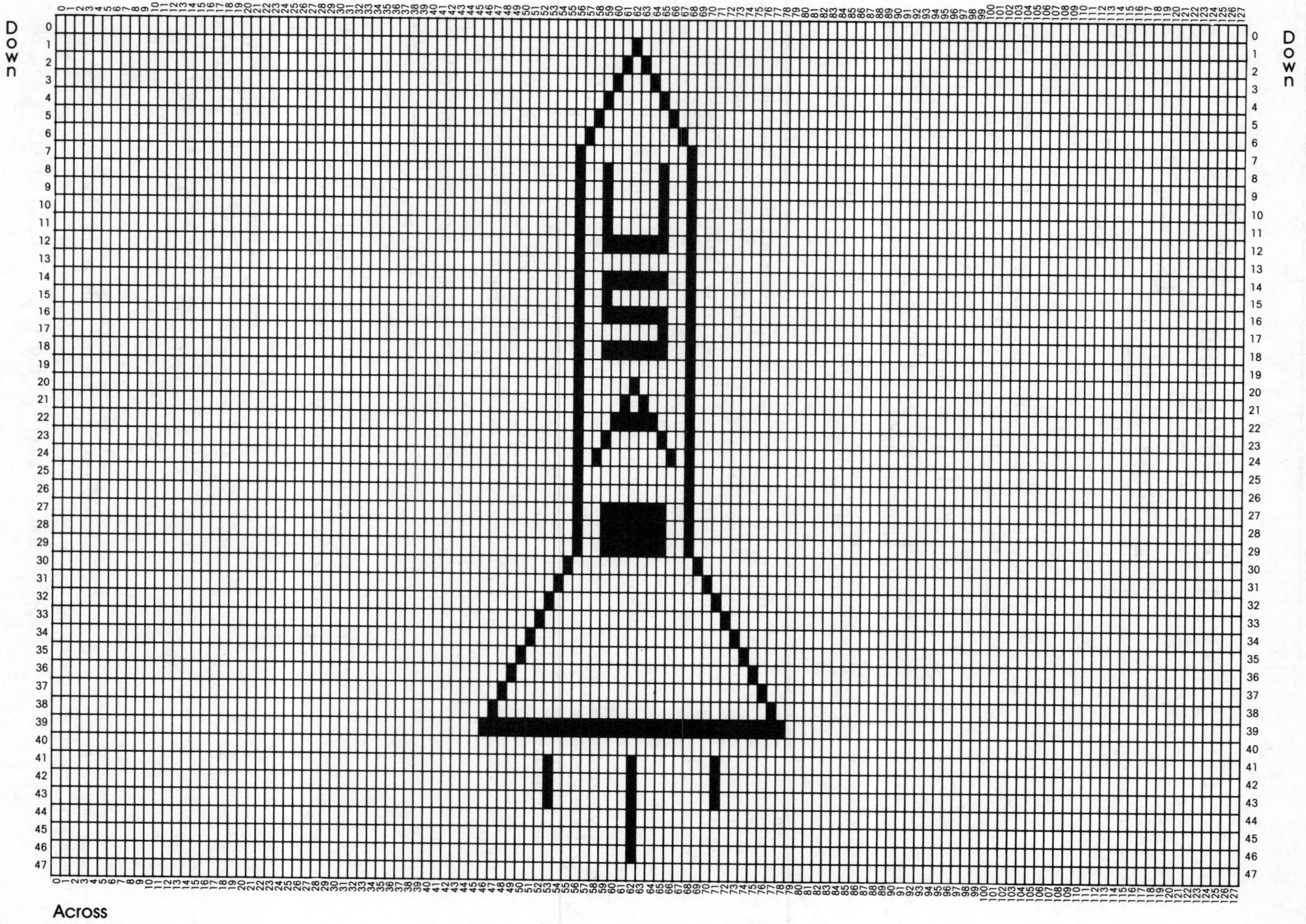

The other side of the spaceship can be programmed the same way.

```
10 FOR D = 7 TO 29
20 SET (68, D)
30 NEXT D
```

Since both sides of the spaceship are the same length, you can use one FOR-NEXT loop to draw them. Instead of having two programs, you can use this program to draw both sides of the ship.

```
10 FOR D = 7 TO 29
20 SET (56, D)
25 SET (68, D)
30 NEXT D
```

The line across the bottom of the spaceship can also be drawn with a FOR-NEXT loop.

```
40 FOR A = 46 TO 78
50 SET (A, 39)
60 NEXT A
```

Find these rectangles on the graph.

This loop draws a line that goes across from 46 to 78. It is located at row 39 (down). The rectangles that make up this line are: (46, 39), (47, 39), (48, 39), . . . (78, 39).

The diagonal lines on the top of the spaceship can be drawn by SETting each individual rectangle.

```
70 SET (62, 1)
80 SET (61, 2)
90 SET (60, 3)
100 SET (59, 4)
110 SET (58, 5)
120 SET (57, 6)
130 SET (63, 2)
140 SET (64, 3)
150 SET (65, 4)
160 SET (66, 5)
170 SET (67, 6)
```

IT'S A LITTLE TIRING TYPING ALL THESE SETS.

HERE'S A SHORTCUT— LOOK BELOW.

There is a way to avoid typing the SETs and parentheses. You can put all the numbers into a DATA statement:

A DATA statement can go anywhere in the program.

```
70 DATA 62, 1, 61, 2, 60, 3, 59, 4, 58, 5, 57, 6, 63, 2, 64, 3, 65, 4, 66, 5, 67, 6, −1, −1
```

Then you can READ the DATA, and SET what you READ.

Line 100 lights up rectangles (62, 1), (61, 2), (60, 3), etc.

```
80 READ A, D
90 IF A = −1 THEN GOTO 120        The data −1, −1 are "dummy" data.
100 SET (A, D)
110 GOTO 80
120                                The program continues.
```

To fill in the box under USA you could draw three horizontal (across) lines:

Find these lines on the graph.

```
120 FOR A = 59 TO 66
130 SET (A, 27)
140 SET (A, 28)
150 SET (A, 29)
160 NEXT A
```

Or, you could use two FOR-NEXT loops. Read this part of the program carefully.

```
120 FOR D = 27 TO 29
130 FOR A = 59 TO 66
140 SET (A, D)
150 NEXT A
160 NEXT D
```

First, 27 is stored in D, and 59 is stored in A. The rectangle at (59, 27) lights up. Then, the next number, 60, is stored in A, and the rectangle at (60, 27) lights up. The program continues in this loop until all the numbers for A are used up. The output is a horizontal line at row 27. Then, the computer goes to the next D, which is 28. The program loops through all the numbers for A. The output is a horizontal line at row 28. Then, the computer goes to the next D, which is 29. The output is a horizontal line at row 29.

When two FOR-NEXT loops are used together, they are called **nested** loops. In the program above, the A loop is nested inside the D loop. In the program below, the D loop is nested in the A loop. This program fills in the same box under USA on the spaceship. It draws 8 short vertical (down) lines from columns 59 to 66.

```
120 FOR A = 59 TO 66
130 FOR D = 27 TO 29
140 SET (A, D)
150 NEXT D
160 NEXT A
```

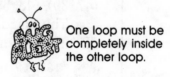 One loop must be completely inside the other loop.

In FOR-NEXT loops, the ⇨ inside loop is done first.

The D loop is nested ⇨ inside the A loop.

Use a graphics sheet ⇨ to help you figure this out.

Don't use numbers larger than 127 across, or larger than 47 down, or you'll get an FC ERROR message. FC stands for "illegal function call." It means you used a number that was too large.

1. Draw the output on a graphics sheet.

```
10 FOR A = 40 TO 90
20 SET (A, 25)
30 NEXT A
```

2. Describe the output for this program.

```
10 FOR A = 0 TO 127
20 FOR D = 0 TO 47
30 SET (A, D)
40 NEXT D
50 NEXT A
```

3. Write a program to draw USA as it appears on the spaceship. Use FOR-NEXT loops to draw the straight lines.

4. Draw your initials on a graphics sheet. If there are any curves, such as in the letter C, you will have to draw them using straight or diagonal lines. Your letters can be any size, large or small. Then, write a program to draw the initials on the computer screen.

168

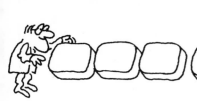

At the Computer

1. Type and run this program.

```
10 FOR A = 0 TO 127
20 SET (A, 24)
30 NEXT A
```

THE STRAIGHT LINE YOU SEE AS THE OUTPUT IS 128 RECTANGLES IN A ROW.

2. Add this line to your program and run it.

```
5 CLS
```

CLS means "clear screen." This line tells the computer to clear the program from the screen. The program is cleared before the output is printed, leaving a clear screen for your computer picture.

3. Change a statement in your program so the computer draws the line at the bottom of the screen.

4. Change a statement in your program so the computer draws the line at the top of the screen. After you run the program, look at what happened to the beginning of the line. The READY message covered it up! The READY message appears when the computer reaches the end of a program. To avoid having part of your graphics blocked out, the program must never end. So, add this statement to your program:

```
1000 GOTO 1000
```

You don't have to use line number 1000. Any line number will do, but it must be the last line in your program.

THAT WILL KEEP THE COMPUTER BUSY. THE PROGRAM WILL NEVER END UNLESS YOU STOP THE COMPUTER.

5. Change a statement in your program so the computer draws a dotted line across the screen. (Hint: Light up every *other* rectangle.)

Type NEW.

6. Write a program to draw your initials. You can use your program from "Try These" exercise 2.

Type NEW.

7. Light up rectangles randomly on the screen. Part of the program is done for you. Complete lines 20, 30, 40, and 50.

This program has an infinite loop. You'll need to stop the computer.

```
10 CLS
20 A = RND( )⌉
30 D = RND( )⌋    Pick the highest number
40 SET ( , )      you want for across and down.
50 GOTO
```

Type NEW.

RESET is a statement that turns off the lighted rectangle.

Type NEW, or change some lines from the previous program.

8. Draw a dot that "moves" across the screen:

```
10 CLS
20 FOR A = Ø TO 127
30 SET (A, 24)
40 RESET (A, 24)
50 NEXT A
60 GOTO 20
```

The dot is not really moving. You are lighting up one rectangle, turning it off, then lighting up the next one, turning it off, and so on.

9. Draw a dot that "moves" *down* the screen.

10. Write a program for the spaceship as it is shown on the graphics sheet. Parts of it have been done for you in "At Your Desk." Also, you programmed the letters in "Try These."

Chapter 24 | ON YOUR OWN

You have learned many statements in BASIC. Not it's time for you to put them together to create your own original program. You may choose to program a computer quiz, a computer ad lib, a computer game, a graphics display, or an animated (moving) picture. You might also have some other ideas.

Before you begin to plan your program, you may want to experiment with a few more statements. Most computers accept these BASIC statements. Check with your teacher or read your computer manual to be sure you can use them.

This program uses a TAB statement. Line 20 tells the computer to indent GOODBYE ten spaces.

TAB is a word in BASIC that means "indent."

```
10 PRINT "HELLO"
20 PRINT TAB(10) "GOODBYE"
RUN
HELLO
                    GOODBYE
```

GOODBYE is printed starting at the tenth space.

Look at this program and output.

```
10 FOR X = 1 TO 3
20 PRINT TAB(X) "HELLO"
30 NEXT X
40 FOR X = 3 TO 1 STEP −1
50 PRINT TAB(X) "GOODBYE"
60 NEXT X
RUN
HELLO
  HELLO
    HELLO
    GOODBYE
  GOODBYE
GOODBYE
```

TAB(X) becomes TAB(1), TAB(2), and TAB(3). HELLO is printed at the first, second, and third spaces.

GOODBYE is printed at the third, second, and first spaces.

The LEFT$ statement indicates characters on the left side of a string. Look at this program and output.

Read LEFT$ as "left-string."

The Atari computer does not use LEFT$, RIGHT$, or MID$ statements.

```
10 A$ = "GOOD"
20 PRINT LEFT$(A$, 3)
RUN
GOO
```
←————Print the **3 left characters** of A$.

You can have fun with the LEFT$ statement.

```
10 A$ = "GOOD"
20 FOR X = 1 TO 4
30 PRINT LEFT$(A$, X)
40 NEXT X
RUN
G
GO
GOO
GOOD
```
←————Print the X left characters of A$. (X changes from 1 to 4.)

The RIGHT$ statement indicates characters on the right side of a string. Look at this program and output.

```
10 A$ = "SUPER!"
20 PRINT RIGHT$(A$, 4)  ←——— Print the 4 right characters of A$.
RUN
PER!
```

The MID$ statement indicates characters in the middle of a string. Look at this program and output.

```
10 A$ = "COMPUTER"
20 PRINT MID$(A$, 3, 2)
RUN
MP
```

MID$(A$, 3, 2)

String Begin at the third position. Print 2 characters.

Here's a way to print one letter at a time on the screen—slowly! To see how the output is printed, you have to try this on a computer.

```
10 A$ = "COMPUTER"
20 FOR X = 1 TO 8
30 PRINT MID$(A$, X, 1)
40 FOR P = 1 TO 50: NEXT P
50 NEXT X
```

Line 30 prints 1 character from A$, starting with position X (X changes from 1 to 8). Line 40 is a time delay.

Getting Started

Here are some hints and guidelines for writing an original program. You can use these ideas along with any of your own ideas. It is important to plan your program carefully. You should know what you want your program to do and what kind of output you want. You might want to write down the main parts of your program and figure out how to program each part. Then you'll be ready to write the statements at the computer.

It is not necessary to write your whole program on paper. Check with your teacher about saving your program on a tape or a disk.

Computer Quiz   You wrote a short computer quiz in Chapter 19. Your new computer quiz should be longer and more interesting. Pick a topic for your quiz and write five to ten questions on that topic. Try to think of different "rewards" for each question. For example, if the user gets the answer right, instead of printing YOU ARE RIGHT, you might try this:

You could also try this:

```
110 FOR X = 1 TO 100
120 PRINT "YOU ARE RIGHT! ";
130 NEXT X
```

```
110 FOR X = 1 TO 12
120 PRINT TAB(X) "YOU'RE RIGHT!"
130 NEXT X
```

You might also want to do a graphics display, such as a smiling face for a correct answer or a frowning face for a wrong answer.

Computer Ad Lib   You wrote a Computer Ad Lib in Chapter 18. This time, make up a short story that is a few sentences long. Underline the key words in your story. For example, one sentence might be: Jeff saw two monkeys swinging on a trapeze.

Next, make up a question for each underlined word. You must also use INPUT statements so the user can answer the questions:

```
10 PRINT "NAME A FRIEND."
20 INPUT F$
```

Then, use print statements to print the ad lib. You must use the address locations instead of the underlined words in this part of the program.

Computer Game   There are many games you can program on the computer. You worked with a number guessing game in Chapter 20. How about typing a letter guessing game? To tell the computer to choose a letter randomly, use MID$:

```
10 A$ = "ABCDEFGHIJKLMNOPQRSTUVWXYZ"
20 N = RND (26)
30 B$ = MID$(A$, N, 1) ◄———— Choose 1 character from position N
                                in the string.
```

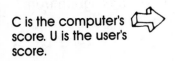
For the Apple, Atari, and PET computers, line 20 is:
N = INT(RND(1)*26) + 1

Now that B$ is the computer's letter, you must compare it to the user's guess. The computer considers the letter A "low" and the letter Z "high." So, A is less than Z, M is greater than D, P is less than Q, and so on. The game is programmed like a number guessing game.

You might want to give your game a name.

Here's another game that's fun to try. Have the computer pick a number randomly (it can be a very large number), and hold it on the screen for a second or less. (Use a FOR-NEXT loop as a time delay.) Then clear the screen and ask the user what the number was. If the user gets the number right, give the user a point. If the user misses the number, give the computer a point. Here's part of a program that keeps score.

C is the computer's score. U is the user's score.

```
110 PRINT "NO, THE NUMBER WAS "; N
120 C = C + 1 ◄————————— The user missed the answer, so
130 GOTO 10                1 is added to the computer's score.
140 PRINT "YOU GOT IT!"
150 U = U + 1 ◄————————— The user was correct, so 1 is
160 GOTO 10                added to the user's score.
```

At the end of the program, print the final score:

```
200 PRINT "YOUR SCORE IS "; U
210 PRINT "MY SCORE IS "; C
```

There are many other kinds of games you might be able to think of. Many games use random numbers.

Graphics Display   To program a graphics display, first draw your picture on a graphics sheet. If your computer has color, mark the color you want each part to be. You can also use random numbers to choose colors or locations on the screen.

Animated Picture   In Chapter 23, Apple, Atari, and TRS-80 computer users programmed a box to "move" across and down the screen. To "move" a larger design, you must draw it, erase it, then draw it in another space on the screen.

CHECKPOINT

Choose the best answer for each.

1. The BASIC command that tells the computer to process a program is

  a. NEW.
  b. GOTO.
  c. RUN.

2. The BASIC command that erases a program from the Random Access Memory is

  a. NEW.
  b. LIST.
  c. RUN.

3. The BASIC command that displays that a program on the screen is

  a. NEW.
  b. GOTO.
  c. LIST.

4. What is the output for:
10 PRINT "6 + 3 = "; 6 + 3

  a. 9
  b. 6 + 3
  c. 6 + 3 = 9

5. 10 PRINT "HELLO"
20 GOTO 10
This program is an example of

  a. a FOR-NEXT loop.
  b. an infinite loop.

6. Choose the correct statement.

  a. LET 3 = N
  b. LET N$ = SHOE
  c. LET N = 3

7. If A = 10 and B = 2, tell the output for: PRINT A*B, A/B

  a. A*B   A/B
  b. 20   5
  c. A*B = 20

8. The statement that tells the computer to stop, print a question mark on the screen, and wait for the user's response is

  a. INPUT.
  b. GOTO.
  c. IF-THEN.

9. What is the output for this program:
10 C = 6
20 IF C = 2 THEN PRINT "RED"

  a. RED
  b. There is no output.

10. Clearing the screen erases a program from the computer's memory.

  a. true
  b. false

11. Which of these statements is used to tell the computer exactly how many loops to make?

  a. FOR-NEXT
  b. IF-THEN
  c. READ-DATA

12. A microcomputer's ability to display pictures and graphs is referred to as

  a. programming.
  b. computer graphics.
  c. text display.

GLOSSARY

abacus

an ancient calculating device consisting of a wooden frame with rods on which beads are moved

Aiken, Howard

an American engineer who designed the first electromechanical computer, the Mark I

analog computer

a computer that measures continuously changing conditions, such as temperature and pressure, and converts them into quantities

algorithm

a step-by-step plan or procedure for solving a problem

Analytical Engine

a mechanical computing device designed, but never completed, by British scientist Charles Babbage in 1835. It was the forerunner of modern digital computers.

arithmetic/logic unit

one of the two main parts of the central processing unit that does calculations and compares numbers

Arithmetic Machine

a calculating machine that could add and subtract; invented by Blaise Pascal in 1642

Babbage, Charles

a British scientist who developed and partially built the Analytical Engine, which was the forerunner of modern digital computers

BASIC

an acronym for Beginner's All-purpose Symbolic Instruction Code. A computer language used in most microcomputers and often used in mainframes and minicomputers.

binary number system

a number system that uses only two digits, 0 and 1

bit

a binary digit, 0 or 1, used to represent the "off" or "on" state of an electric circuit. It is the smallest unit of digital information a computer processes.

bug

any mistake in a computer program

byte

a unit usually made up of 8 bits. One byte represents one character on the computer keyboard.

card reader

an input device that transfers data from punched cards to the computer's memory

cassette tape

a strip of magnetic material on which computer programs are stored in the form of magnetic impulses. Used with a tape recorder as an I/O device for microcomputers.

cathode ray tube (CRT)

see *video screen*

central processing unit (CPU)

the part of a computer system that processes information. Its two main parts are the arithmetic/logic unit and the control unit.

character

a letter, number, or symbol found on a computer keyboard

chip

see *integrated circuit chip*

circuit

a path through which electricity flows

COBOL

an acronym for Common Business Oriented Language. A computer language used for business applications.

command

a word (in BASIC) that usually tells the computer to do something with a program. For example, RUN is a command.

computer

a machine designed to accept information, store information, process information, and give out processed information

computer engineer

a person who designs circuitry used in computer systems

computer operator

a person who runs a computer, particularly a mainframe

computer technician

a person who repairs computers. A technician also works with an engineer in designing a computer.

concatenate

a word that means "to link together." In programming, strings can be concatenated.

control unit

one of the two main parts of the central processing unit. It directs the flow of information through a computer system.

cursor

the symbol appearing on the video screen that shows where the next character to be typed will appear

data

information. Also refers to information that is to be input or information that is the output of a program.

data bank

a collection of computerized information that is usually stored on I/O storage devices such as tapes and disks

data processing

taking data, or information, that has been input and using it to produce information in other forms such as reports

digit

a single number from 0 through 9

digital computer

a general-purpose computer that uses letters, numbers, and symbols as input and converts this information into digits to be stored and processed

disk

a flat, circular device with a magnetic surface that is capable of storing computer programs. Some disks are flexible (see *floppy disk)* and some are hard (see *hard disk)*

disk drive

an I/O device that loads a program or data stored on a disk into a computer

dummy

a variable of piece of data in a program which has no special meaning itself

Eckert, J. Presper

an American engineer who, with John Mauchly, designed the ENIAC and UNIVAC computers

electromechanical

made with both electric and mechanical (moving) parts

ENIAC

an acronym for Electronic Numerical Integrator and Calculator. The first electronic computer designed by Eckert and Mauchly in 1946.

floppy disk

a magnetic storage device commonly used with microcomputers

FORTRAN

an acronym for FORmula TRANslator. A programming language commonly used for scientific and engineering applications

graphics

non-text designs and patterns displayed as output

hard copy

paper output from a printer; printout

hard disk

a magnetic storage device commonly used with minicomputers and mainframes

hardware

computer machinery

Hollerith, Herman

an American engineer who designed the Tabulating Machine, which used punched cards to sort data from the 1890 census

infinite loop

a set of instructions that continuously repeat in a program

information retrieval

one function of a computer that deals with sorting out requested information from a large set of stored data

input

information to be put into the computer

input device

part of a computer system that puts information into the computer's memory. It is sometimes referred to as an *input unit*

input/output device

a device that functions as an input and an output device

integrated circuit (IC)

an electrical pathway, made up of many transistors, that transmits electricity much faster than a single transistor. Integrated circuits were used in third-generation computers.

integrated circuit chip (ICC)
a very tiny wafer of silicon containing thousands of integrated circuits. Chips are used in fourth-generation computers.

I/O
refers to input/output

Jacquard, Joseph
a French weaver who, in 1801, designed a loom which used punched cards to store patterns that were woven into fabric

K
stands for *kilo* or 1,000; used when referring to memory size, such as 16K bytes

keyboard
an input device used for typing data

keypunch machine
a machine used to punch holes in cards, which are used for computer input

keypunch operator
a person who operates a keypunch machine

large scale integration (LSI)
the process of putting thousands of integrated circuits on one silicon chip

Leibniz, Gottfried
a German scientist who, in 1694, built a calculating device called the Stepped Reckoner

light pen
an input device, resembling a pen, that responds to light on the video screen

Lovelace, Ada Augusta
an English mathematician who assisted Charles Babbage in designing the Analytical Engine and who wrote about Babbage's work

magnetic ink character recognition (MICR)
a kind on input in which a MICR reader interprets characters printed with special magnetic ink

mainframe computer
a large computer system that can handle many jobs at once

Mark I
the first electromechanical computer. It was designed by Howard Aiken in 1944.

Mauchly, John

an American engineer who, with J. Presper Eckert, designed the ENIAC and UNIVAC computers

memory

the part of a computer system that stores information

microcomputer

a small desktop computer that can do one job at a time. It is also called a *home* or *personal computer*.

minicomputer

a medium-size computer system which can do several jobs at once

nanosecond

one billionth of a second. It is used to measure computer speed.

Napier, John

a Scottish mathematician who, in 1612, invented the calculating device known as Napier's Bones

Napier's Bones

a set of numbered rods, developed by John Napier, which was used for calculating

optical mark reader

an input device that reads pencil markings on paper

output

the results of a processed program

output device

the part of the computer system that displays, prints, or records the results. It is sometimes referred to as an *output unit*.

PASCAL

a computer language, named after Blaise Pascal, used in microcomputers as well as larger systems

Pascal, Blaise

a French mathematician who invented the Arithmetic Machine in 1642

password

a code word (or number) that must be entered into a computer before the user can access a program or other data

peripheral equipment

hardware, such as tape recorder or printer, that is connected to the main computer

plotter
>an output device that draws pictures and graphs on paper

printer
>an output device that prints output on paper

printout
>the output from a printer. It is also called *hard copy*.

process control
>using a computer to control specified jobs or conditions, such as temperature

program
>a set of instructions, written in a computer language, that tells a computer what to do

programmer
>a person who writes computer programs

prompt
>a symbol used by some computers to indicate when the computer is ready to accept input

punched card
>a paper card containing holes that stand for data or programs

punched card loom
>weaving machine, perfected by Joseph Jacquard in 1801, which used punched cards to store patterns that were woven into fabric

Random Access Memory (RAM)
>the computer's temporary memory. It stores data and programs that are input.

Read Only Memory (ROM)
>the computer's permanent memory.

read/write head
>a device inside a disk drive that reads information on a disk. It can also "write" and erase information.

reel-to-reel tape
>a kind of I/O storage

robot
>a special-purpose computer designed to perform mechanical tasks

scanner
>an input device usually used to read Universal Product Codes on packaged products.

scientific notation

a shorthand for very large or very small numbers. On a computer, 6.987E+09 stands for 6,987,000,000.

silicon

a common element in the earth's crust from which computer chips are made

simulation

a computerized output which imitates a real-life situation

software

programs for a computer. Usually refers to programs stored on devices such as disks or tapes.

software librarian

a person in charge of large collection of software in a company

statement

a word (in BASIC) that gives an instruction and is used in a program

Stepped Reckoner

a calculating machine, invented by Gottfried Leibniz in 1694, that could add, subtract multiply, and divide

string

any combination of letters, numbers, or symbols (except quotation marks)

syntax error

an error in the structural rules of a programming language. It is usually an error in spelling or punctuation.

systems analyst

a person who analyzes a situation and designs a computerized system to handle it

Tabulating Machine

a machine, designed by Herman Hollerith in 1887, which counted and recorded data from punched cards. It was used to tabulate results of the 1890 U.S. census

tape drive

an I/O device that reads and stores data on magnetic tape

tape recorder

an I/O device commonly used with microcomputers

terminal

an I/O device that has a keyboard for input and either a video screen or a printer for output. It is connected to a mainframe or minicomputer.

text

refers to numbers, letters, or keyboard symbols (as opposed to graphics)

transistor

a device used to transmit electricity in second-generation computers

UNIVAC

an acronym for UNIVersal Automatic Computer. It was designed by Eckert and Mauchly in 1951 and was the first commercial computer

Universal Product Code (UPC)

a series of bars and numbers printed on packaged grocery goods. A UPC is read by scanner in a computerized checkout system.

user

a person who is using a computer program

vacuum tube

a device used to transmit electricity in first-generation computers

video screen

an output device used to display information. It is also referred to as a *cathode ray tube (CRT)* or *monitor.*

voice synthesizer

an output device which translates computer output into human-like sounds

von Neumann, John

an American mathematician who introduced the idea of storing a program in first-generation computers

word processing

the ability of a computer to allow the user to move or change words, sentences, and paragraphs without retyping them

INDEX

Abacus, 37
Accounts, 54
Addresses, 97-104
Aiken, Howard, 44
Algorithm, 80
Analog computers, 58
Analytical Engine, Babbage's, 40-41, 44
Apollo 13, 52
Apostrophe, 89
Apple computer graphics, 148-152
Arithmetic Machine, Pascal's, 39
Arithmetic unit, 24-26
Atari computer graphics, 152-159

Babbage, Charles, 40-41
Banks, computers in, 57-58
BASIC, 9, 78
　writing in, 78-79
BASIC programming, 75-174
Bi, prefix, 33
Bills, computerized, 53
Binary digits, 33
Binary number system, 33, 40
Bits, 33
Bugs, 79
Bytes, 33

CAI (Computer Assisted Instruction), 60-61
Calculating, 83-84
Capital (upper-case) letters, 74
Card reader, 14-15
Cards
　Hollerith, 41
　punched, 14-15, 40, 41
Careers, computer, see Computer careers
Cassette tape, 13
Cassette tape recorder, 10, 13
Cathode ray tube (CRT), 17
Census, 41
Census Bureau, 51

Central processing unit, 5-7, 10, 24-28
Characters
　inverse, 163
　magnetic, 16
Chinese abacus, 37
Chips
　actual-size, 48
　computer, 29-32, 48-49, 61-62
　enlarged, 30, 48
　integrated circuit (ICCs), 29-32, 48-49, 61-62
Circuit, 30, 47
Circuit board, computer, 29
Circuits, integrated, 47-49
COBOL, 9
Colon (:), 121, 163
COLOR, 153
Comma (,), 86-87
Command, 81
Commercial computer, 46
Computer ad lib, 172-173
Computer art, 148-170
Computer Assisted Instruction (CAI), 60-61
Computer careers, 69-72
　with computer hardware, 70-71
　with computer software, 69-70
　computer-related careers, 71-72
Computer chips, 29-32, 48-49, 61-62
Computer development, 37-49
　ancient times, 37-38
　1600s, 38-39
　1800s, 40-43
　modern computers, 44-49
Computer engineers, 70-71
Computer game, 173
Computer graphics, see Graphics
Computer keyboard, 75-79
Computer languages, 9
Computer "mistakes," 53-54
Computer operators, 71
Computer quiz, 172
Computer-related careers, 71-72
Computer speed, 25

Computer systems, 1-4
Computer teachers, 72
Computer technicians, 71
Computer uses, 51-68
　in banks, 57-58
　crime and, 67-68
　in factories, 56-57
　in government, 51-52
　in homes, 61-62
　in hospitals, 58-59
　in newspapers, 59-60
　in offices, 53-54
　privacy and, 64-67
　in schools, 60-61
　in supermarkets, 54-56
　in the space program, 52-53
　types of, 62-63
Computerized bills, 53
Computerized X-ray machines, 58
Computers
　analog, 58
　communicating with, 8-11
　digital, 44-45
　electromechanical, 44-45
　first-generation, 45-46, 49
　fourth-generation, 48-49
　future generations of, 49-50
　mainframe, 1-3
　Mark I, 44
　modern, four generations of, 44-49
　parts of, 5-7
　personal, 46
　"personal" and "home", 3
　pocket-size, 49
　second-generation, 47, 49
　third-generation, 47-48, 49
Concatenate, 107, 110
Confidential files, 66
Control unit, 26-28
Copy, hard, 18, 71
CPU (central processing unit), 5-7, 10, 24-28
Credit bureau, 64-65

Crime, computers and, 67-68
CRT (cathode ray tube), 17
Cursor, 77

Data, 15, 20
DATA, 142-147, 167
Data banks, 64-65
Data processing, 62-63
Deca, prefix, 37
Decimal number system, 33, 37
Decisions, computer, 118-126
Digital computers, 44-45
Digits, 37
  binary, 33
DIM, 106
Disk drive, 10, 13-14
Diskettes, 13
Disks
  floppy, 13
  hard, 14
Division sign, 90
Dollar sign ($), 105
DRAWTO, 153
"Dummy" number 128

E for "exponent," 104
Eckert, J. Presper, 45
Electromechanical computer, 44-45
END, 81
Engineers, computer, 70-71
ENIAC, 45-46
ENTER, 76
Error, syntax, 78
Exponent, E for, 104

Factories, computers in, 56-57
First-generation computers, 45-46,
  49
Floppy disks, 13
FOR-NEXT, 135-140, 168
FORTRAN, 9
Fourth-generation computers, 48-49

GOTO, 91-96
Government, computers in, 51-52
Graphics, 148
  Apple computer, 148-152

Atari computer, 152-159
  PET computer, 160-164
  TRS-80 computer, 165-170
Graphics text, 156
GRAPHICS (GR.), 152-159
Greater than (>), 119-121

Hard copy, 18, 71
Hard disk drive units, 14
Hardware, 10
  careers with, 70-71
HLIN, 150
Hollerith, Herman, 41
Hollerith cards, 41
HOME, 151
"Home" computers, 3
Homes, computers in, 61-62
Hospitals, computers in, 58-59

IF-THEN, 118-126
Infinite, 95
Infinite loop, 93, 101, 128
Information
  personal, 65
  retrieving, 44
  stored, 20
Information retrieval, 62
Input, 10
INPUT, 111
Input devices, 12
  peripheral, 13
Input/output devices, 19
Input unit, 5-7, 10
INT, 129
Integer, 129
Integrated circuit chips (ICCs), 30,
  48-49, 61-62
Integrated circuits, 47-49
Integration, large scale (LSI), 30
Internal Revenue Service, 51, 66
International Business Machines
  (IBM), 42
Inventory, 54
Inverse character, 163
I/O devices, 19

K (kilo), 34

Keyboard, 12
  computer, 75-79
  TRS-80, 75
Keypad, 74
Keypunch machine, 14
Keypunch operators, 69

Languages, computer, 9
Large scale integration (LSI), 30
LEFT$, 171
Leibniz, Gottfried Wilhelm von, 39
Less than (<), 119-121
LET, 98-104
Librarians, software, 69-70
Light pen, 16
Line number, 81
LIST, 21, 88
Logic unit, 25
Loop
  FOR-NEXT, 135-140, 168
  infinite, 93,101, 128
  nested, 168
Lovelace, Lady Ada Augusta, 40-41

Machine, keypunch, 14
Magnetic characters, 16
Magnetic ink character recognition
  (MICR) reader, 15, 57
Mainframe computers, 1-3
Mark I computer, 44
Mauchly, John W., 45
Memory, 20-23
  Random Access (RAM), 20-22, 23
  Read Only (ROM), 20-22, 23
  16K, 34
Memory units, 5-7, 10
MICR (magnetic ink character
  recognition) reader, 15, 57
Microcomputers, 1, 3-4
Microprocessors, 32
MID$, 172
Minicomputers, 1, 2-3
Multiplication symbol, 90

Nanoseconds, 25, 27, 34
Napier, John, 38
Napier's Bones, 38
NASA, 4

Nested loops, 168
NEW, 20, 22, 94
Newspapers, computers in, 59-60
NEXT, 135-140
Notation, scientific, 104
Number system
    binary, 33, 40
    decimal, 33, 37
Numbers
    "dummy," 128
    line, 81
    random, 127-134
    stored, 110-102
    zero and one, 33

Offices, computers in, 53-54
One, number, 33
Operators, computer, 71
Optical mark reader, 15
Output, 10
Output devices, 17-19
Output unit, 5-7, 10

PASCAL, 9
Pascal, Blaise, 38
Passwords, 68
Peripheral input devices, 13
"Personal" computers, 3
PET computer graphics, 160-164
PLOT, 150, 153
Plotters, 18, 30
PRINT, 9, 80-90
    with nothing after it, 115
Printer, 18
Printout, 18, 86
Privacy, computers and, 64, 67
Process, 10
Process control, 63
Processing, 6
Programmers, 69
Programming, BASIC, 75-174
Programs, 9, 80
    tracing, 81
Prompt, 77
Public relations, 71-72
Punched-card loom, Jacquard's, 40
Punched cards, 14-15, 40, 41
Punctuation marks, using, 85-87

Quotation marks, 79, 81, 83, 90, 99

RAM (Random Access Memory),
    20-22, 23, 97
Random Access Memory (RAM),
    20-22, 23, 97
Random numbers, 127-134
READ, 142-147, 167
Read Only Memory (ROM), 20-22, 23
Reader
    card, 14-15
    magnetic ink character
        recognition (MICR), 15, 57
    optical mark, 15
Reel-to reel tape drives, 14
RESET, 170
Retrieving information, 44
RETURN, 76
RIGHT$, 172
RND, 127-134
Robots, 56-57
ROM (Read Only Memory), 20-22, 23
RPG, 9
RUN, 9, 21, 81

Sales representatives, 71
Scanners, 55
Schools, computers in, 60-61
Scientific notation, 104
Screen, video, 17
Second-generation computers, 47,
    49
Semicolon (;), 85-87, 96
SET, 165
SETCOLOR, 154-155
SHIFT, 76, 163
Silicon, 30
Simulation, 63
Software, 11, 69
    careers with, 69-70
Software librarians, 69-70
Space bar, 76
Space program, computers in, 52-53
Speed, computer, 25
Statements, 81
STEP, 136-137
Stepped Reckoner, Leibniz's, 39
Stored information, 20
Stored numbers, 100-102

Strings, 105-110
Supermarkets, computers in, 54-56
Switch, on-off, 77
Syntax error, 8, 78
Systems analysts, 70

TAB, 171
Tabulating Machine, Herman
    Hollerith's 41-42
Tape drives, reel-to-reel, 14
Tape recorder, cassette, 10, 13
Teachers, computer, 72
Technical writers, 72
Technicians, computer, 71
Telephone connections, 1, 2
Terminals, 1, 2, 3, 12, 59
Text, 148
    graphics, 156
Third-generation computers, 47-48,
    49
Time delays, 141-147
Tracing a program, 81
Transistors, 47
TRS-80 computer graphics, 165-170
TRS-80 keyboard, 74

UNIVAC, 46
Universal Product Code (UPC),
    55-56
Upper-case (capital) letters, 74
Users, 111

Vacuum tubes, 45, 47
Video screen, 17
VLIN, 150
Voice synthesizers, 49
Von Neumann, John, 466

Word processing, 59-60
Writers, technical, 72
Writing in BASIC, 78-79

Zero
    number, 33, 74
    slash through the number, 9
Zones, 86